Navigating the New Era:

Unraveling the Dynamics of Leadership and Management for Future-Proof Success

Dato Nikoleishvili

Table of Contents

Dedication/Acknowledgments

With every stride you take toward progress, there will always be someone who harbors envy and ill intentions toward you. However, this adversity serves as fuel for your inner strength. As I moved towards the pinnacle of my professional journey, I found myself faced with a situation where these individuals sought to ensnare me in a trap, hoping to hinder my advancement.

I had dedicated my heart and soul to my fast-paced career, yet their actions compelled me to embark on a different path. Through their attempt to set a trap, these individuals unknowingly propelled me toward an entirely new direction.

Instead of succumbing to anger and hatred, which are one's greatest adversaries, I am genuinely grateful to these misguided souls who unintentionally played a significant role in shaping my new profession.

There is a saying that when one door slams shut, you must seek out another to open. And if that door is locked as well, my dear reader, then climb through the window!

I wholeheartedly extend my forgiveness and empathy towards those individuals, for their malicious intentions have boomeranged back to them, leaving them in a pitiful state.

1

I want them to understand that I am always prepared to offer my assistance should they require my support.

It is with great honor that I dedicate this book to those individuals, and I sincerely wish for them to conquer their egos and rediscover their true selves.

Introduction

Leadership and management have been studied throughout history; different scholars have tried to describe what they mean, and we have experienced an evolution of their meaning. I hope to inform my readers about the numerous changes in leadership and management, especially after the COVID-19 pandemic.

It is vital to understand the minute variations in successful leadership and management styles today and eliminate outdated notions. However, I want to introduce myself before discussing what is in the book.

I am the founder and director of LLC Nix Development, a property development company in Tbilisi, Georgia. Our latest project involves the construction of an eight-story residential structure in Tbilisi.

My farm, located in the Kakheti region, Georgia, covers a large land area and is managed by my company, LLC Eastern Gardens: Almond Gardens. The farm produces high-quality almonds that are sold both domestically and internationally.

My third business venture is the USA-based Corporation, which is a transportation logistics company. The company specializes in providing ground freight transportation services for clients, helping them move cargo across the land.

Beyond my business ventures, I have extensive experience in different fields, such as educational business and the energy industry. The biggest experience I have gained is in the public sector, primarily in the security forces. I have held various roles in Georgia's Ministry of Internal Affairs from 2000 to 2017, including a top inspector, head of the division, Head of the LEPL-Service Agency, and Chief of the Mia Border Police.

As a Ph.D. researcher in the business and economics department at Tbilisi State University, my interests include exploring the distinctions between leadership and management in the public and commercial spheres.

I am thrilled to share with my dear readers the remarkable combination of my real-world experience and academic expertise. It is a captivating convergence that I am eager to impart to all of my readers. Therefore, prepare yourself for an extraordinary voyage of educational exploration and self-discovery by fastening your seatbelt.

This book will delve deep into the distinctions between leadership and management in the public and commercial spheres, highlighting the significant changes that have taken place in contemporary society. I have intended this book for a broad audience, including business professionals, academics, students, and anyone interested in leadership and management.

This book challenges the traditional view that leadership and management are synonymous and demonstrates the distinct nature between the two. By providing readers with a clear understanding of the differences between leadership and management and the various ways these concepts are applied, the book will equip them with the knowledge and tools they need to become influential leaders and managers in their respective fields.

Chapter 1:

Understanding Leadership & Management

L eadership and management are the terms often used interchangeably in the business world. However, despite their similarities, they are fundamentally distinct concepts that require different skills and approaches. In this chapter, we will explore the differences between leadership and management, highlighting the unique roles and responsibilities of each. Let's start with concept of management.

Management involves organizing and directing resources to achieve specific goals, and it includes tasks such as:

- Planning
- Organizing
- Controlling
- Directing resources

The core purpose is to ensure that organizational objectives are met optimally. Managers are responsible for ensuring that day-to-day operations run smoothly and tasks are completed on time and within budget. They are also accountable for managing resources such as people, finances, and technology to ensure they are employed effectively and efficiently.

However, management is not just about overseeing processes and completing tasks. It also involves motivating and leading people to achieve their full potential. Managers must be skilled in communication, team building, and conflict resolution to ensure their teams are productive and engaged. They must be able to provide guidance and direction to their team members, ensuring that everyone is aligned toward a common goal.

Leadership is focused on inspiring and motivating people to achieve a shared vision. Leaders are responsible for setting the direction and goals of an organization and inspiring their teams to achieve them. Unlike managers, who focus on achieving specific objectives, leaders are concerned with creating a vision for the future and inspiring others to follow that vision.

Leaders must be skilled in communication, motivation, and visioning. They must be able to communicate their vision in a way that inspires and motivates others to follow them. They must also build strong relationships with their team members, creating a culture of trust and collaboration that encourages creativity and innovation.

The Ship Metaphor:

One way to understand the difference between leadership and management is to consider the metaphor of a ship. The ship's captain is like a manager, responsible for ensuring that the ship is on course, that the crew follows the right procedures, and that the ship is maintained and repaired as necessary. The captain focuses on the ship's day-to-day operations, ensuring it stays afloat and moves in the right direction.

On the other hand, the ship's navigator is like a leader. The navigator is responsible for setting the ship's course, deciding where it should go and how it should get there. The navigator is focused on the big picture, ensuring that the ship is headed in the right direction and arrives at its destination safely and on time.

The Differences Between the Two:[1]

There is certainly an overlap between leadership and management. Management involves overseeing processes, resources, and people to achieve specific objectives, while

---

[1] Nizarudin Wajdi, Muh. (2017). The Differences Between Management And Leadership. Sinergi : Jurnal Ilmiah Ilmu Manajemen. 7. 10.25139/sng.v7i1.31.

leadership is about inspiring and guiding others toward a shared goal.

Managers focus on efficiency, structure, and control, using systems and processes to optimize performance and minimize risks. They are responsible for planning, organizing, and directing an organization's resources to achieve specific outcomes. In contrast, leaders are focused on vision, inspiration, and innovation. They encourage creativity and collaboration, creating a sense of purpose that inspires others to work toward a shared goal.

One key difference between management and leadership is the way they motivate people. Managers typically use extrinsic motivators like rewards and punishments to encourage people to perform well. In contrast, leaders rely more on intrinsic motivators like personal fulfillment, a sense of purpose, and a desire to contribute to something greater than oneself. While both approaches can be effective in different situations, research suggests that intrinsic motivation is more sustainable and leads to greater job satisfaction and performance over the long term.

Another key difference is the way they handle change. Managers tend to be more risk-averse, focusing on maintaining stability and avoiding disruption. They often ensure existing systems and processes work effectively and efficiently. On the other hand, leaders are more comfortable with change and disruption, recognizing that innovation and growth often require taking risks and challenging the status quo. They are responsible for setting a direction for the organization, aligning people around a common vision, and inspiring them to take action.

Of course, it is important to recognize that management and leadership are critical components of any successful organization. Without effective management, an organization can quickly become disorganized and chaotic; without strong leadership, it can lack direction and purpose. The key is to find the right balance between the two and to recognize that they are complementary rather than mutually exclusive.

Leadership and Management Today:

In contemporary society, both leadership and management are critical for the success of organizations. The Covid-19 pandemic has highlighted the importance of effective leadership and management in navigating through uncertain times. Leaders must inspire and motivate their team members, communicate a vision that inspires confidence, and make decisions that ensure the organization's survival. Managers must ensure that resources are allocated efficiently, deadlines are met, and the team works together to achieve the set goals.

The role of leaders and managers has evolved, and contemporary society requires leaders and managers who can adapt to changing circumstances. The digital age has brought about new challenges and opportunities, and leaders and managers must be skilled at navigating this rapidly changing landscape. They must leverage technology to drive innovation and increase efficiency while maintaining a human touch that inspires confidence and fosters collaboration.

In today's business environment, successful leadership and management styles have evolved significantly, reflecting the complexity of the modern workplace, changing demographics, and evolving expectations of employees and customers. The chapter analyzes these changes and highlights the variations in successful leadership and management styles today.

One of the most significant changes in leadership and management practices today is the increasing focus on diversity and inclusivity. Organizations with a more diverse workforce must embrace different leadership styles that reflect their employees' needs and expectations. For example, a more participatory leadership style that involves collaboration and inclusivity may be more effective in engaging diverse teams than traditional top-down approaches.

Another key trend in successful leadership and management styles today is the shift towards a more agile and adaptable approach. In today's fast-paced and rapidly changing business environment, leaders and managers must be able to pivot quickly and adapt to new situations. This requires a flexible approach that emphasizes experimentation, innovation, and risk-taking. Leaders willing to take calculated risks and learn from their mistakes are more likely to succeed in today's dynamic business environment.

Additionally, there is a growing emphasis on the importance of emotional intelligence in leadership and management practices. Emotional intelligence is the ability to effectively understand and manage one's emotions and those of others. Leaders and managers with high emotional intelligence can better connect with their employees, build trust and rapport, and create a positive workplace culture that fosters collaboration and creativity.

Finally, there is a growing recognition of the importance of sustainability and corporate social responsibility in successful leadership and management practices.

Customers and employees alike are increasingly concerned about the impact of businesses on the environment and society. Organizations prioritizing sustainability and social responsibility are more likely to attract and retain top talent, build strong relationships with their customers, and enhance their reputation in the marketplace.

Effective leaders and managers must adapt to changing circumstances, leverage technology to drive innovation and increase efficiency, and maintain a human touch that inspires confidence and fosters collaboration. By understanding the distinctions between leadership and management, organizations can ensure they have the right people in the right roles to achieve their goals and succeed in a rapidly changing world.

Evolution of management:

Leadership and management practices have undergone significant changes over time. Various factors, including technological advancements, globalization, and social, economic, and political changes, have influenced these changes. Understanding their historical context and how they have evolved is essential to understand the current state of leadership and management practices.

Historically, management practices were focused on maximizing efficiency and productivity. The scientific management approach, developed by Frederick Winslow Taylor in the early 20th century, was based on the idea that work processes could be broken down into individual tasks that could be optimized for efficiency. This approach emphasized standardization, measurement, and control, and it was widely adopted by organizations seeking to improve their productivity.[2]

In the mid-20th century, the focus of management shifted to a more humanistic approach, emphasizing the importance of human relations and motivation. This approach was influenced by researchers such as Abraham Maslow and Douglas McGregor, who emphasized the importance of employee needs and motivations. This led to the development of management theories such as Theory X and Theory Y, which emphasized the importance of creating a positive work environment and engaging employees to improve productivity.[3]

---

[2] Scientific Management Theory Explained. Villanovau.com. (2022). Retrieved from
https://www.villanovau.com/resources/leadership/scientific-management-theory-explained/
[3] Kurt, D. S. (2022, October 17). Theory X and theory Y, Douglas McGregor. Education Library. Retrieved from
https://educationlibrary.org/theory-x-and-theory-y-douglas-mcgregor/

Evolution of leadership:

Leadership practices have also evolved. Historically, leadership was viewed as a position of authority and power, with leaders expected to provide direction and make decisions for their subordinates. However, in the mid-20th century, the focus of leadership shifted towards a more collaborative and participatory approach. This approach emphasized the importance of involving employees in decision-making and empowering them to take ownership of their work, which led to the development of leadership theories such as situational leadership, which emphasized the importance of adapting leadership styles to the needs of individual employees and situations.

The Great Man Theory:

The great man theory emerged in the 19th century, maintaining that leaders are born instead of trained or made. The theory supported that only a few people possess leadership qualities and gave examples.[4]

This concept evolved into the trait theory, meaning leaders could be made through practice and training.

[4] Organ, D. W. (1996). Leadership: The great man theory revisited. Business Horizons, 39(3), 1–4. https://doi.org/10.1016/s0007-6813(96)90001-4

However, the trait theory didn't catch on as the required characteristics weren't identified.[5]

Behavioral Theory:

The trait theory led to behavioral theory, which focused on the leader's behavior instead of their traits or qualities. Based on this theory, researchers have identified various behavioral patterns grouped and labeled as leadership styles. This approach gained popularity in management training, with the Blake and Mouton Managerial Grid being a prominent example. Today, leadership development programs emphasize acquiring leadership skills and behaviors, supporting that leadership can be acquired through learning.[6]

Situational or Contingency Theory:

With time, it became clear that the environment played a significant role in the leader-follower dynamic. Leaders needed to assess the situation and choose the most appropriate style, making this approach known as the contingency theory of leadership.

---

[5] Buchanan, D. A., & Huczynski, A. (2019). Organizational behaviour. Pearson.

[6] Denison, D. R., Hooijberg, R., & Quinn, R. E. (1995). Paradox and performance: Toward a theory of behavioral complexity in managerial leadership. Organization Science, 6(5), 524–540. https://doi.org/10.1287/orsc.6.5.524

Fred Fiedler was one of the pioneers of contingency theory, stressing the importance of context in effective leadership. He believed there is no ideal set of leadership traits or behaviors but that a leader's fixed style must be matched with the appropriate situation. Essentially, a leader's effectiveness depends on how well their leadership style aligns with their context.[7]

Transactional Theory:

In the late 90s, researchers recognized leadership cannot be studied on a single dimension. Leaders need to change quickly, incorporate new technologies, and understand the interaction between the situation, employees, and the environment.

This innovative mindset led to the transactional theory of leadership. The transactional theory follows a managerial style by motivating employees by focusing on goals and rewarding them. Effective leaders would not delay rewarding and recognizing their employees' efforts and

[7] Fiedler, F. E., & Chemers, M. M. Leadership and Effective Management (Glenview, 111.: Scott, Foresman, 1974); David R. Hampton et al., Organizational Behavior and the Practice of Management, 4th ed.(Glenview, 111.: Scott, Foresman, 1982), 571-575.

achievements. Transactional leadership works best in manufacturing, sales, and situations with strict deadlines.[8]

Transformational Theory:

The transformational leadership style is based on four components:

- Intellectual Stimulation
- Individual Consideration
- Inspirational Motivation
- Idealized Influence

Transformational leaders prioritize nurturing and motivating their employees, encouraging creativity and independence rather than micromanagement. This leadership style is particularly effective for organizations focused on employee development and innovation rather than immediate productivity or sales goals. It can also be valuable in new or innovative industries where creative thinking is essential for success.[9]

Today, leadership and management practices continue to evolve in response to changing social, economic, and political conditions. The Covid-19 pandemic has

---

[8] Hollander, E. P., & Offermann, L. R. (1990). Power and leadership in organizations: Relationships in transition. American Psychologist, 45(2), 179–189. https://doi.org/10.1037/0003-066x.45.2.179

[9] Bass, B. M., & Riggio, R. E. (2014). Transformational leadership. Routledge.

highlighted the importance of flexibility, adaptability, and resilience in leadership and management practices. As organizations adapt to new ways of working, leaders and managers must be able to respond quickly and effectively to changing conditions.

Understanding the historical context of leadership and management practices is vital to know how they will likely evolve. By understanding the evolution of these practices, leaders and managers can gain valuable insights into what worked and what is likely to work. They can also identify areas where current practices may need to be adapted or improved to meet changing conditions.

Efficient Leaders and Managers in Organizations:

Throughout this chapter, we have established that leadership and management are two concepts often used interchangeably but are fundamentally distinct. While both are essential for the success of any organization, they require different skills and approaches.

Effective leadership involves setting a vision, motivating and empowering team members, and creating a positive culture that promotes innovation and growth. Leaders must communicate effectively, build relationships, and make sound decisions aligning with the organization's goals and values.

On the other hand, management is the process of planning, organizing, directing, and controlling resources to achieve specific goals. Managers oversee day-to-day operations, allocate resources, and ensure that projects are completed on time and within budget. Effective management requires strong organizational skills, attention to detail, and coordinating teams to achieve specific outcomes.

To be successful, organizations need both strong leaders and effective managers. Leaders provide direction, inspiration, and vision, while managers ensure that the organization's resources are allocated and utilized effectively. While some people are natural leaders, others can learn to become effective leaders through training and development.

Similarly, management skills can be developed through training and experience. Many organizations provide management training programs that teach key skills such as planning, organizing, and delegating tasks. Effective managers must communicate effectively, build relationships, and motivate their teams to achieve specific goals.

So far, we have briefly touched upon leadership and management's similarities and differences and their theories and evolution. As we proceed with chapters, you will learn about these aspects in detail. By the end of this book, you will understand the differences between these two concepts and learn how one can become an effective leader and manager and contribute to the success of their organization.

Chapter 2:

The Similarities & Differences

So far, we have established that management and leadership are interrelated concepts essential to any organization's success.

Management can be defined as the process of planning, organizing, leading, and controlling resources, including people, finances, and technology, to achieve organizational goals. The primary focus of management is to ensure the efficient and effective use of resources to accomplish the organization's objectives. The characteristics of management include being task-oriented, analytical, and process-driven. Managers are responsible for setting goals, allocating resources, developing strategies, and monitoring performance. They also play a critical role in ensuring that the organization complies with regulations and standards.

On the other hand, leadership can be defined as the ability to inspire and motivate people to achieve a common goal. Leadership is about influencing others to take action and achieve success together. The focus of leadership is on people and their development, as well as creating a vision and setting direction for the organization. The characteristics of leadership include being people-oriented, visionary, and inspirational. Leaders are responsible for creating a positive culture, developing talent, and fostering innovation.

In modern times, the definitions of management and leadership have become more nuanced, reflecting the evolving nature of work and the increasing complexity of organizational challenges. Today, management is not just about maintaining the status quo and ensuring efficiency. Instead, managers must be agile, adaptable, and innovative to navigate the rapidly changing business landscape. They need to anticipate and respond to disruptions and leverage technology to create new opportunities.

Similarly, leadership has taken on a broader perspective in contemporary times. Leaders need to be able to think strategically and to drive change. They must communicate effectively, build relationships, and empower their teams to achieve their full potential. In addition, leaders need to navigate complex stakeholder relationships and balance different groups' needs.

This chapter will discuss more similarities, differences, roles, skills, and responsibilities.

Similarities Between Management & Leadership:

Management and leadership are two essential functions that are crucial in any organization. They play a significant role in determining the success or failure of a business. Today's society is characterized by a dynamic and fast-paced environment, which demands a different approach to management and leadership.

Effective organizations need both management and leadership to achieve their goals. Understanding the similarities and differences between these two concepts is crucial for anyone in a position of responsibility within an organization.

Empathy and Emotional Intelligence:

Emotional intelligence is becoming increasingly important in today's society, particularly in leadership positions. Leaders and managers must understand and manage their emotions effectively and their teams. They must be empathetic and able to connect with their team on a human level. Emotional intelligence enables leaders to build trust and create a positive work environment. They must ensure that their team is not lacking motivation or going through anxiety, burnout, or depression.

Visionary Thinking:

Leaders must have the ability to think beyond the immediate future and have a clear vision of where they want the organization to be in the long term. They must articulate this vision to their team and inspire them to achieve it.

Shared Purpose:

Both management and leadership involve creating a shared purpose that inspires and motivates individuals toward a common goal.

People-Centric:

Both management and leadership involve working with people and understanding their needs and motivations to create an environment that fosters productivity and growth.

Decision Making:

Both management and leadership involve making important decisions that affect the organization's success.

Adaptability:

Leaders must be adaptable and flexible in their approach to management and be able to change course quickly when needed. They must be willing to experiment with new ideas and be open to feedback from their team.

Collaboration:

Managers and leaders must be able to work collaboratively with their teams to achieve shared goals.

They must create a culture of collaboration where everyone feels valued and has a voice in decision-making. Managers and leaders who prioritize collaboration are better able to navigate the complex challenges of the present.

Technology Savviness:

Technology has become an integral part of business operations nowadays. Leaders must be tech-savvy and understand the latest technologies and trends. They must leverage technology to improve efficiency, productivity, and overall performance — leaders who are not tech-savvy risk falling behind the competition and becoming irrelevant.

Diversity and Inclusion:

Leaders must be committed to creating a diverse and inclusive workplace where everyone feels valued and included. They must actively work towards eliminating bias and promoting equity in their organization. Leaders prioritizing diversity and inclusion can better attract and retain top talent and build a strong reputation.

Appreciating employees:

A report by Harvard Business Review concluded recognition given to high performers impacted the employee's drive the most.[10] Appreciation boosts employee morale and aligns productive resources with the organization's goals. Such leaders and managers have a strong following, and their departments produce excellent results.

Dealing with Conflicts:

Conflicts are a part of any team, as competition, grudges, and different working styles exist. Effective managers identify conflicts timely and try their best to alleviate the situation.

Open to feedback:

Feedback is necessary for growth, and managers should be open to feedback from their juniors and seniors. In a good environment, employees feel free to try innovative ideas and give feedback to existing ones.

Employee Development:

Every employee wants to grow, and if their managers and leaders guide them, they will become more productive than ever. Good leadership knows their team's strengths and weaknesses and develops programs that work on weaknesses while enhancing the strengths.

---

[10] Harvard Business Review. (rep.). The Impact of Employee Engagement on Performance. Retrieved from https://hbr.org/resources/pdfs/comm/achievers/hbr_achievers_report_sep13.pdf.

There are several other similar characteristics that managers and leaders possess. Some of them are below:[11]

- **Innovation:** The ability to generate new ideas and take calculated risks to pursue growth and success.
- **Purpose:** A strong sense of purpose and values that guide decision-making and actions.
- **Agility:** The ability to adapt quickly to change and to pivot in response to new challenges.
- **Focus:** Leaders and managers focus on progress and result at the same time.
- **Time Management:** They track projects' deadlines and their teams' efficiency. Great leaders delegate tasks appropriately and get the work done on time.

Differences Between Management and Leadership

Focus:

The primary focus of management is to maintain the status quo and ensure that day-to-day operations are running smoothly. On the other hand, the primary focus of leadership is to create a vision for the future and inspire individuals to work towards it.

---

[11] Randall J. Beck and Jim Harter. (2023, April 19). Why great managers are so rare. Gallup.com.
https://www.gallup.com/workplace/231593/why-great-managers-rare.aspx

Direction:

Management often focuses on maintaining control and ensuring employees follow established procedures and protocols. Conversely, leadership involves setting direction and creating a roadmap for achieving the organization's goals.

Approach:

Management is often associated with a more bureaucratic and hierarchical approach, while leadership is associated with a more democratic and collaborative approach. Management is often more directive, with managers providing clear instructions and guidelines to employees. Conversely, leadership is often more collaborative, with leaders working closely with employees to achieve shared goals.

Influence:

Management relies on positional power and the authority of a job title. In contrast, leadership depends on influence and the ability to inspire and motivate others toward a shared vision.

Time Horizon:

Management often has a short-term focus, while leadership focuses on the organization's long-term vision.

Risk:

Management is often risk-averse and focuses on minimizing risk, while leadership involves taking calculated risks to achieve the organization's goals.

Roles of Leaders and Managers:

The primary role of a manager is to plan, organize, and control resources to achieve specific objectives. They are responsible for creating and implementing policies and procedures, setting budgets, allocating resources, and supervising employees. Managers are accountable for the success of their teams and are expected to make decisions that optimize the use of resources.

On the other hand, leaders are responsible for creating a vision and inspiring people to work towards that vision. They are responsible for setting the organization's tone, culture, and direction. Leaders create a sense of purpose, direction, and meaning and motivate people to work towards achieving the shared goal.

Skills of Leaders and Managers:

The skills required for effective management include planning, organizing, decision-making, problem-solving, delegation, communication, and interpersonal skills. Managers must be able to manage budgets, timelines, and resources effectively while also being able to communicate effectively with employees, clients, and stakeholders.

The skills required for effective leadership include vision, creativity, empathy, communication, and interpersonal skills. Leaders must inspire and motivate people to work towards a shared goal, create a sense of purpose and direction, and build strong relationships with employees, clients, and stakeholders.

Responsibilities of Leaders and Managers:

The primary responsibility of a manager is to ensure that the organization's resources are used effectively and efficiently to achieve specific objectives. Managers are responsible for making decisions that optimize the use of resources, managing budgets, timelines, and resources, and ensuring that employees perform at their best.

Leaders are responsible for creating a vision for the organization and inspiring people to work towards that vision. They are responsible for building a culture of innovation, creativity, and collaboration and empowering employees to achieve their full potential.

A Mix of Leadership and Management:

It is important to note that while management and leadership are distinct concepts, they are not mutually exclusive. Effective managers often exhibit leadership qualities, such as setting a vision and inspiring their team, while effective leaders often rely on management skills, such as organizing and controlling resources. In many organizations, the roles of manager and leader overlap, and individuals are expected to exhibit both skills.

Effective management requires a range of skills, including strong communication, organizational, and problem-solving skills. Managers need to be able to plan, delegate, and supervise tasks effectively. They must also adapt to changing circumstances and make decisions quickly. Additionally, they need to manage conflict and build strong relationships with their team members.

Effective leadership, on the other hand, requires a different set of skills. A leader needs to inspire and motivate people to achieve their best work. They need to be able to communicate their vision and goals effectively and build a sense of trust and loyalty within their team. They must also be able to take calculated risks, innovate, and adapt to changing circumstances. Additionally, leaders must manage conflict and build strong relationships with their team members.

While management and leadership are different, both are necessary for organizational success. They complement each other and work together to achieve common goals. Managers provide stability and continuity, while leaders provide inspiration and direction. Together, they ensure that the organization can adapt to changing circumstances, take advantage of new opportunities, and remain competitive.

Organizations need to have strong management and strong leadership to be effective. This requires a commitment to ongoing training and development of both sets of skills. It also requires a willingness to empower and support both managers and leaders to take risks, innovate, and drive change.

While management and leadership have different approaches and goals, both are necessary for organizational success. Effective management requires different skills from effective leadership, but both are equally important. Organizations that recognize and develop both sets of skills will be better equipped to adapt to changing circumstances, innovate, and achieve their goals.

Chapter 3:

Theories on Leadership

L et's dive into different leadership theories and see what makes these theories ideal for becoming a contemporary leader. Traditional notions of leadership have given way to contemporary approaches that emphasize adaptability, collaboration, and empowerment. You will read about contemporary leadership theories and styles, gaining insights into the diverse strategies that leaders can adopt to inspire and guide their teams.

Transformational Leadership:

Transformational leadership is a highly influential and widely recognized contemporary theory focusing on the leader's ability to inspire and motivate followers to achieve exceptional results. This leadership style goes beyond transactional exchanges and instead emphasizes transforming individuals and organizations.

At the core of transformational leadership is the leader's capacity to create a compelling vision that resonates with the values and aspirations of their team members. By articulating a clear and inspiring vision, transformational leaders provide a sense of direction and purpose, instilling in their followers a shared understanding of the organization's goals and objectives. This vision serves as a guiding force, aligning the team's efforts toward a common goal.

Transformational leaders possess exceptional communication skills and use persuasive abilities to communicate the vision effectively. They engage in open and honest dialogue, actively listening to the concerns and ideas of their team members. Through their communication, they create an atmosphere of trust and transparency, fostering a sense of ownership and commitment among their followers.

These leaders also act as role models by setting high standards of performance and behavior. They lead by example, exhibiting the values and behaviors they expect from their followers. Transformational leaders demonstrate integrity, honesty, and ethical conduct, earning the trust and respect of their team members. Their actions serve as a source of inspiration, motivating others to emulate their behavior and strive for excellence.

Significantly, transformational leaders invest in their followers' personal and professional development. They provide guidance and support, helping individuals identify their strengths and weaknesses and offering growth opportunities. By recognizing and nurturing the potential of their team members, transformational leaders empower them to achieve their full potential, fostering a culture of continuous learning and improvement.[12]

Servant Leadership:

Servant leadership is another influential theory focusing on the leader's commitment to serving others. Leaders who adopt this style prioritize the needs of their team members, emphasizing empathy, humility, and active listening. Servant leaders foster trust, collaboration, and engagement by supporting their employees' development and well-being. They seek to build strong relationships and enable their team to reach their full potential.

Servant leadership is a powerful and influential theory emphasizing the leader's commitment to serving others.

---

[12] Ugochukwu, C., & Chioma (2023, May 19). Transformational leadership theory: How to inspire and motivate. Simply Psychology. https://www.simplypsychology.org/what-is-transformational-leadership.html

Unlike traditional leadership models that often revolve around the leader's authority and power, servant leadership flips the paradigm by prioritizing the needs of team members and supporting their growth and well-being. This approach recognizes that leaders can succeed by empowering and enabling those they lead.

At the heart of servant leadership lies the genuine concern for others. Leaders who adopt this style have a deep understanding of their team members' aspirations, challenges, and strengths. They actively listen to their employees, seeking to understand their perspectives, needs, and goals. By demonstrating empathy, servant leaders create an environment where individuals feel valued, respected, and heard.

Humility is another crucial characteristic of servant leadership. Leaders who exhibit humility recognize that they are not infallible and that they can learn from others. They acknowledge the contributions of their team members and are not afraid to admit their mistakes or seek guidance. This humility fosters trust and openness within the team, as individuals feel comfortable sharing their ideas, opinions, and concerns without fear of judgment.

Servant leaders are also committed to the development and well-being of their team members. They invest time and effort into understanding their employees' strengths and areas for growth. They support their team's professional and personal development through mentorship, coaching, and resources. Servant leaders create growth opportunities, challenging their team members to stretch their abilities and reach their full potential.

Building solid relationships is a cornerstone of servant leadership. These leaders prioritize creating a culture of collaboration and trust, fostering an environment where individuals feel safe to take risks, share their thoughts, and contribute their unique perspectives. Servant leaders build a cohesive, high-performing team aligned to achieve shared goals by promoting teamwork and encouraging open communication.

Servant leadership also encompasses the idea of enabling and empowering others. Rather than micromanaging or controlling their team members, servant leaders provide the necessary resources, support, and autonomy for individuals to succeed. They trust their team's abilities and delegate responsibilities, allowing individuals to take ownership of their work and make meaningful contributions. This empowerment leads to increased team engagement, creativity, and innovation.[13]

Authentic Leadership:

Authentic leadership is a leadership style that strongly emphasizes leaders being true to themselves and acting in alignment with their core values. Authentic leaders are genuine, transparent, and self-aware, which enables them to build trust and establish meaningful connections with their team members. By embodying authenticity, these leaders create an environment that fosters open communication, encourages collaboration, and empowers employees to bring their best selves to work.

One of the critical characteristics of authentic leadership is the consistency between words and actions. Authentic leaders understand the importance of practicing what they preach. They lead by example, ensuring that their behaviors align with the values and principles they espouse. This consistency builds credibility and trust among team members, who can rely on their leader to be genuine and reliable.

---

[13] Kenton, W. (2022, October 8). Servant leadership: Characteristics, Pros & Cons, example. Investopedia. https://www.investopedia.com/terms/s/servant-leadership.asp

Authentic leaders also prioritize transparency in their communication. They are open and honest with their team members, sharing information and insights openly. This transparency helps to create a culture of trust and openness, where employees feel comfortable expressing their ideas and concerns without fear of judgment or reprisal. Authentic leaders promote creativity, innovation, and collaboration by fostering a psychological safety climate.

Self-awareness is a fundamental trait of authentic leaders. They deeply understand their strengths, weaknesses, values, and emotions. This self-awareness allows them to make conscious decisions, respond effectively to challenges, and regulate emotions in difficult situations. By being self-aware, authentic leaders are better equipped to understand the impact of their actions on others and can make more informed decisions that consider the well-being of their team members.

Authentic leadership also emphasizes the importance of building meaningful connections with team members. Authentic leaders genuinely care about the personal and professional growth of their employees. They invest time and effort in getting to know their team members individually and understanding their aspirations, strengths, and development needs. Authentic leaders create a sense of belonging by building these connections and fostering a positive and supportive work environment.

In addition to creating a positive work environment, authentic leaders promote ethical behavior. They uphold high moral standards and demonstrate integrity in their actions. Ethical leadership is a guiding compass for authentic leaders, ensuring that decisions and actions are aligned with ethical principles. Authentic leaders cultivate a culture of integrity, trust, and respect by setting an honest tone and holding themselves and others accountable.[14]

Situational Leadership:

Situational leadership is a dynamic and flexible approach that recognizes the ever-changing nature of leadership. This theory emphasizes that there is no one-size-fits-all leadership style, as a leader's effectiveness depends on their ability to adapt their approach to different situations and the unique needs of their followers. Leaders who embrace situational leadership understand that individuals within their team possess varying levels of competence, commitment, and expertise.

The core principle of situational leadership lies in the leader's capacity to assess and understand their team

---

[14] Gavin, M. (2019, December 10). Authentic leadership: What it is & why it's important: HBS Online. Business Insights Blog. https://online.hbs.edu/blog/post/authentic-leadership

members' readiness or developmental level. Readiness combines an individual's competence and commitment to perform a specific task or achieve a particular goal. Competence refers to the knowledge, skills, and abilities required to complete a task, while commitment refers to an individual's motivation, confidence, and willingness to take on responsibilities.

Based on this assessment, situational leaders can adjust their leadership style along a continuum that ranges from high directive-low supportive behaviors to low directive-high supportive behaviors. When followers are less competent and committed, leaders may adopt a more directive approach, providing specific instructions and clear guidelines and closely monitoring their progress. This approach helps to build confidence and develop competence among team members who may be new to a task or lack experience.

Conversely, leaders can shift toward a more supportive role when followers demonstrate high competence and commitment. They provide encouragement, empower individuals to make decisions, and offer guidance when needed. This approach allows team members to take ownership of their work, fostering a sense of autonomy and promoting further growth and development.

One of the critical benefits of situational leadership is its adaptability. Leaders who practice this style can modify their behavior and leadership approach as the situation evolves or as team members' readiness levels change. This adaptability enables leaders to provide the proper support and guidance, ensuring that individuals receive the appropriate resources and direction to succeed in their tasks.

However, it is essential to note that situational leadership requires leaders to deeply understand their team members' strengths, weaknesses, and development needs. Practical assessment and continuous monitoring of individuals' readiness levels are essential for successfully applying this theory. Leaders must also possess the necessary skills to adjust their leadership style flexibly and provide the appropriate direction and support.[15]

Distributed Leadership:

Distributed leadership is a contemporary leadership theory that recognizes the potential for leadership to emerge from various levels within a team or organization. Unlike traditional hierarchical structures where leadership

[15] Cherry, K. (2023, March 10). Why the most effective leaders know how to adapt to the situation. Verywell Mind. https://www.verywellmind.com/what-is-the-situational-theory-of-leadership-2795321

is concentrated at the top, distributed leadership acknowledges that expertise, skills, and leadership qualities can be found throughout the organization. This approach challenges the notion of a single leader and encourages the distribution of leadership responsibilities among individuals.

In a distributed leadership model, individuals are empowered to take on leadership roles based on their unique skills, knowledge, and experience. This decentralization of leadership allows for a more inclusive and collaborative approach, where team members are actively involved in decision-making processes and contribute to the organization's overall success.

One of the key benefits of distributed leadership is that it taps into the diverse talents and perspectives within the organization. Distributed leadership promotes innovation and creativity by recognizing and harnessing the expertise of individuals at all levels. Different team members bring unique insights and ideas, leading to more robust and effective problem-solving and decision-making. This collaborative environment fosters continuous learning and improvement, as individuals are encouraged to share their knowledge and contribute to the organization's collective wisdom.

Moreover, distributed leadership encourages accountability and ownership among team members. When individuals are given leadership responsibilities, they are more likely to take ownership of their work and strive for excellence. This shared leadership approach creates a sense of collective responsibility, where each team member understands their role in achieving organizational goals and is motivated to contribute their best efforts.

Implementing distributed leadership successfully requires a supportive organizational culture. Leaders must create an environment that fosters trust, open communication, and collaboration. This includes establishing clear channels for information sharing, encouraging teamwork and cross-functional collaboration, and recognizing and valuing the contributions of individuals at all levels.

However, it is essential to note that distributed leadership does not imply a complete absence of formal leadership roles. While leadership responsibilities are distributed, individuals may still hold formal leadership positions, providing overall guidance and direction. These leaders are critical in creating an organizational structure that enables distributed leadership to thrive.[16]

Ethical Leadership:

Ethical leadership is a critical and influential leadership style that strongly emphasizes moral values, integrity, and social responsibility. Leaders who adopt this style uphold ethical principles and hold others accountable for their actions, creating a culture of ethical behavior within the organization. Ethical leaders foster trust, credibility, and long-term sustainability by establishing a robust ethical framework.

One of the key characteristics of ethical leaders is their unwavering commitment to moral values. They make decisions and take actions that align with honesty, fairness, respect, and transparency. Ethical leaders serve as role models for their followers, consistently demonstrating ethical behavior in their interactions and decision-making processes.

Moreover, ethical leaders understand the importance of holding themselves accountable. They acknowledge their mistakes, take responsibility for their actions, and strive to learn and grow from those experiences. By taking

---

[16] Kennedy, S., Abdulai, A.-M., & Siobhan. (2018, January 24). Distributed leadership explained. Home. https://www.sec-ed.co.uk/best-practice/distributed-leadership-explained/

ownership of their behavior, they inspire others to do the same and create a culture of personal responsibility and accountability.

In addition to personal accountability, ethical leaders promote a culture of responsibility within the organization. They establish clear expectations and standards of behavior, ensuring that everyone understands the ethical guidelines they should adhere to. When ethical violations occur, ethical leaders address them promptly and fairly, sending a strong message that unethical behavior will not be tolerated.

Ethical leaders create trust and credibility among their followers by fostering an environment built on ethics. Employees feel secure knowing their leaders act with integrity and have their best interests at heart. This trust and credibility lead to increased employee engagement, loyalty, and commitment to the organization's goals.

Furthermore, ethical leadership has a profound impact on long-term organizational sustainability. By prioritizing moral values, leaders create a foundation for ethical decision-making at all levels of the organization. This, in turn, reduces the risk of ethical breaches, scandals, and legal issues. Organizations led by ethical leaders are more likely to attract and retain top talent, build strong relationships with stakeholders, and maintain a positive reputation in the marketplace.

Ethical leadership serves as a guiding compass for ethical decision-making. When faced with complex choices, leaders can refer to their ethical framework to make decisions that consider the welfare of all stakeholders and align with the organization's values. This ethical decision-making process ensures that the organization operates in a socially responsible and sustainable manner.

Ultimately, ethical leadership fosters a culture of integrity throughout the organization. It encourages open communication, ethical discussions, and a commitment to doing what is right, even when faced with challenges or temptations. This culture of integrity permeates all aspects of the organization's operations and influences the behavior of its employees, contributing to its overall success and positive impact on society.[17]

Autocratic Leadership:

Autocratic leadership is characterized by centralized control and decision-making authority held by a single individual or a small group of leaders. In this style, leaders

---

[17] Western Governors University. (2020, February 4). What is ethical leadership?. Western Governors University. https://www.wgu.edu/blog/what-is-ethical-leadership2001.html

exercise significant power over their subordinates without much input or participation from the team. They make decisions independently, issue directives, and expect obedience and compliance.

Autocratic leaders can make swift decisions, avoiding delays associated with seeking consensus or gathering input from others. This leadership style establishes a transparent chain of command, providing a structured framework within the organization. Autocratic leaders can effectively manage crises by taking immediate control and providing clear directives.

There are also some downsides; by limiting team members' input, autocratic leadership may stifle creativity and innovative thinking within the organization. Employees may feel demotivated and undervalued due to limited involvement in decision-making processes. The autocratic style often leads to high turnover rates as employees seek more participatory and empowering work environments.[18]

---

[18] Cherry, K. (2023, February 27). What are the pros and cons of autocratic leadership?. Verywell Mind.
https://www.verywellmind.com/what-is-autocratic-leadership-2795314

Democratic Leadership:

Democratic leadership emphasizes the involvement of team members in decision-making processes, allowing for shared input and collaborative problem-solving. In this style, leaders encourage open communication, respect diverse perspectives, and foster a sense of inclusiveness.

Democratic leaders promote exchanging ideas, leading to a broader range of solutions and fostering a culture of innovation. By involving employees in decision-making, democratic leadership empowers individuals, fostering a sense of ownership and job satisfaction. Participatory decision-making processes increase engagement, as employees feel valued and influential.

Some disadvantages also exist; for example, the democratic style can be slower due to the inclusion of multiple perspectives and the need for consensus-building, potentially leading to delays. When quick decisions are required, democratic leadership may face challenges in providing immediate direction due to the emphasis on collective decision-making. Inclusion of diverse perspectives can lead to conflicts if not managed effectively, requiring strong conflict resolution skills from leaders.[19]

---

[19] Cherry, K. (2023, April 6). Is Democratic leadership the best style of leadership? Verywell Mind.

Laissez-Faire Leadership:

Laissez-faire leadership involves minimal leader interference, giving team members considerable freedom to make decisions and manage their work. Leaders in this style provide minimal guidance and rely on the expertise and self-motivation of their subordinates.

Laissez-faire leadership allows individuals to explore their creativity and exercise autonomy in decision-making, fostering a sense of ownership and self-motivation. This leadership style can inspire innovative approaches and solutions to challenges by providing freedom and flexibility. Laissez-faire leadership allows individuals to take on more responsibility and develop their skills and expertise.

On the other hand, without clear guidance, some team members may struggle with decision-making and coordination, resulting in confusion and inefficiency. Without strong oversight, individuals may not feel accountable for their actions, decreasing productivity and performance. Laissez-faire leadership is most effective when team members possess the necessary skills, experience, and self-discipline to work independently.[20]

---

https://www.verywellmind.com/what-is-democratic-leadership-2795315

[20] Cherry, K. (2022, November 14). What are the effects of laissez-faire leadership?. Verywell Mind.

Some Real Life Examples of Leadership

Business Leadership:

In the world of business, exceptional leaders possess the ability to guide organizations to unprecedented heights. One notable example is Steve Jobs, the co-founder of Apple Inc. Jobs exemplified a transformational leadership style, emphasizing innovation and inspiring his team to push boundaries. By fostering a culture of creativity and focusing on customer-centric design, he revolutionized the technology industry, resulting in groundbreaking products like the iPhone and iPad.

Jobs' visionary approach to leadership was evident in his emphasis on customer-centric design. He believed in creating products to meet customer needs and exceed their expectations. Under his guidance, Apple revolutionized multiple industries, introducing groundbreaking products like the iPhone, iPad, and iPod, which reshaped how we communicate, consume media, and interact with technology. Jobs' transformative leadership style left an indelible mark on Apple's culture, emphasizing excellence, attention to detail, and a relentless pursuit of perfection.[21]

---

https://www.verywellmind.com/what-is-laissez-faire-leadership-2795316

[21] Isaacson, W. (2014, October 29). The real leadership lessons of Steve Jobs. Harvard Business Review.

Political Leadership:

Political leaders face unique challenges in guiding nations and shaping policies. One prominent example is Nelson Mandela, the former President of South Africa. Mandela embodied the principles of authentic leadership, demonstrating unwavering integrity and a commitment to justice and reconciliation. His ability to unite a divided nation and dismantle apartheid peacefully serves as a testament to the power of ethical leadership.

Mandela's leadership style is authentic, characterized by his ability to inspire and mobilize others through his personal values and moral compass. Throughout his life, Mandela consistently displayed integrity, remaining steadfast in his convictions and refusing to compromise on equality and human rights principles. His unwavering commitment to these values helped him earn the trust and respect of his supporters and adversaries.[22]

Another noteworthy leader is Angela Merkel, the former Chancellor of Germany. Merkel exhibited a democratic leadership style, emphasizing collaboration and

---

https://hbr.org/2012/04/the-real-leadership-lessons-of-steve-jobs

[22] MATHUR-HELM. D. B., & ANDERSON, J. (2015, December 1). Mandela: The art of the authentic leader. London Business School. https://www.londcn.edu/think/the-art-of-the-authentic-leader

consensus-building. Her steady leadership during times of economic crisis and her compassionate approach to handling the refugee crisis showcased the effectiveness of inclusive decision-making and empathetic leadership.

Through her leadership, Merkel fostered an open dialogue and collaboration environment, encouraging diverse perspectives and ensuring that decision-making processes were inclusive. Her ability to build consensus and find common ground helped Germany navigate complex political landscapes and address societal challenges effectively.[23]

Sports Leadership:

In sports, effective leadership can inspire teams to achieve extraordinary feats. One such example is Sir Alex Ferguson, the legendary former manager of Manchester United Football Club. Ferguson's leadership style combined transformational and autocratic elements, demanding excellence while fostering loyalty and motivation among his players. Under his guidance,

---

[23] Gaspar, F. H. (2022, August 9). Looking at Angela Merkel's leadership style through the Leipzig Leadership Model I HHL blog. HHL Leipzig Graduate School of Management. https://www.hhl.de/blog/merkels-leadership-crisis-shows-the-woman/

Manchester United achieved unparalleled success, winning numerous domestic and international titles.[24]

Additionally, Serena Williams, a renowned tennis player, demonstrates leadership qualities on and off the court. Known for her resilient mindset and dedication to continuous improvement, Williams embodies the traits of a charismatic leader. She has become a role model for aspiring athletes worldwide through her perseverance and determination.[25]

Aspiring leaders can draw inspiration from these real-life examples, understanding how theories and styles can be adapted and integrated into their leadership journeys. By studying and reflecting upon successful leaders' experiences, individuals can cultivate their unique leadership styles, honing their abilities to motivate, inspire, and guide others toward shared goals. Applying leadership theories and styles in real-life situations is the cornerstone of achieving sustainable success and lasting impact in any field.

---

[24] Mohamed, N. (2016, June 25). 5 successful traits that business leaders can take from sir Alex Ferguson. GBNews.ch | Actualités: Emploi, RH, économie, entreprises, Genève, Suisse. https://www.gbnews.ch/5-successful-traits-that-business-leaders-can-take-from-sir-alex-ferguson/
[25] Segal, E. (2022, August 22). Leadership lessons from retiring tennis star Serena Williams. Forbes. https://www.forbes.com/sites/edwardsegal/2022/08/20/leadership-lessons-from-retiring-tennis-star-serena-williams/?sh=4646e8f771f9

Chapter 4:

Evolution of Leadership

Once considered a rigid and hierarchical concept, leadership has undergone a remarkable transformation over the past few decades. Gone are the days of command and control, replaced by a more inclusive, adaptable, and inspiring style of leading. Today, leadership is not confined to the walls of a corner office but thrives on collaboration, empathy, and a shared vision. This chapter will discuss the remarkable evolution of leadership and the qualities that make modern leaders genuinely impactful.

From Authority to Empowerment:

Previously, leaders held positions of authority and were regarded as the sole decision-makers within their organizations. They wielded power and directed their subordinates without much consideration for their input or ideas. This traditional hierarchical approach to leadership often resulted in limited creativity, stifled innovation, and a lack of employee engagement.

However, the dawn of the 21st century brought about significant changes in how organizations operate and succeed. The complex and interconnected nature of today's globalized world demanded a shift in leadership paradigms. Leaders realized that to thrive in this new landscape, they needed to empower individuals and foster a culture of trust, collaboration, and ownership.

Modern leaders understand that their role is not to dictate every decision or micromanage their team members. Instead, they recognize that their true success lies in creating an environment that encourages unleashing their team's potential. They believe in the power of collective intelligence and understand that diverse perspectives and ideas fuel innovation and drive organizations forward.

Empowering individuals means providing them with autonomy and the freedom to make decisions. It involves delegating responsibility and trusting in the abilities and expertise of team members. When leaders empower their teams, they foster a sense of ownership and accountability. This, in turn, boosts employee morale, motivation, and commitment.

In addition to empowering individuals, modern leaders understand the importance of fostering a culture of trust within their organizations. Trust is the foundation for effective collaboration and teamwork. When employees trust their leaders and feel trusted in return, they are more likely to take risks, express their ideas, and contribute wholeheartedly to the organization's success.

Furthermore, modern leaders recognize that empowerment is not a one-time event but an ongoing process. They invest in the development of their team members, provide coaching and mentorship, and create growth opportunities. By fostering a learning culture and supporting continuous skill development, leaders ensure their team members are equipped to handle challenges and seize opportunities in an ever-evolving landscape.

Empowerment-driven leadership is not without its challenges. It requires leaders to let go of control, overcome their egos, and embrace the collective wisdom of their teams. It demands effective communication and the ability to set clear expectations and goals. However, the benefits far outweigh the challenges. Leaders unlock their team's potential, foster creativity and innovation, and empower individuals by creating an inclusive and engaging work environment.[26]

---

[26] Smet, A.D., Hewes, C. and Weiss, L. (2020) For smarter decisions, empower your employees, McKinsey & Company.

Collaboration and Teamwork:

The days of the lone wolf leader, making decisions in isolation and dictating orders, are long gone. Instead, successful leadership now recognizes the power of harnessing the collective potential of a diverse team.

The challenges we face in the modern era are often intricate and multifaceted, requiring a range of perspectives, expertise, and skill sets to address effectively. Recognizing this, current leaders have honed their ability to build teams encompassing various talents and backgrounds. They understand that assembling individuals with complementary skills and experiences creates a fertile ground for innovation and problem-solving.

Moreover, modern leaders foster an environment where open communication thrives, and every voice is valued. They recognize that each member brings a unique perspective and valuable insights into a team. By encouraging active participation and fostering a culture of psychological safety, leaders empower their team members to freely share their thoughts, ideas, and concerns. They understand that diverse viewpoints lead to richer discussions and better decision-making.

Available at: https://www.mckinsey.com/capabilities/people-and-organizational-performance/our-insights/for-smarter-decisions-empower-your-employees

Furthermore, modern leaders go beyond simply assembling a team; they actively foster collaboration among team members. They create structures and processes that promote cross-functional collaboration and encourage sharing of knowledge and resources. By breaking down silos and promoting a sense of collective responsibility, leaders ensure that the combined efforts of their team yield more significant results than the sum of individual contributions.

Collaboration and teamwork are not just about the practical benefits of combining expertise; they also create a sense of belonging and camaraderie within the team. Modern leaders understand the importance of cultivating strong relationships among team members. They foster a supportive and inclusive culture where trust and respect are the foundation for collaboration. By nurturing these connections, leaders create an environment where individuals are motivated to work together, support one another, and celebrate collective achievements.[27]

Leaders who embrace collaboration and teamwork unlock a world of possibilities. They leverage the collective

---

[27] Teamwork and collaboration: How to improve both at work. indeed.com. (2023, February 28).
https://www.indeed.com/career-advice/career-development/teamwork-and-collaboration

intelligence of their teams to drive innovation, creativity, and problem-solving. When individuals from diverse backgrounds come together, they bring fresh perspectives and alternative approaches, allowing for more comprehensive and robust solutions.

Moreover, collaboration enables teams to navigate challenges with agility and adaptability. In a rapidly changing world, responding quickly and effectively is crucial. Leaders and their teams can pool their resources, skills, and knowledge to address unexpected obstacles and seize new opportunities by working collaboratively.

Emotional Intelligence:

Emotional intelligence has emerged as a cornerstone of effective leadership, reshaping how leaders interact with their teams and fostering a more positive and productive work environment. In the past, the traditional image of a leader was often associated with toughness and emotional detachment. However, the evolving leadership landscape has highlighted the importance of empathy, self-awareness, and understanding and managing emotions.[28]

---

[28] Landry, L. (2019, April 3). Emotional intelligence in leadership: Why it's important. Business Insights Blog.
https://online.hbs.edu/blog/post/emotional-intelligence-in-leadership

Leaders with high emotional intelligence possess a remarkable capacity to connect with others on a deeper level. They are genuinely interested in their team members' thoughts, feelings, and concerns. By listening actively and empathizing with their employees, these leaders create an atmosphere of trust and psychological safety. When individuals feel seen and heard, they are more likely to express their ideas, share their concerns, and contribute to the team's success.

Self-awareness is another vital aspect of emotional intelligence in leadership. Leaders who possess self-awareness clearly understand their strengths, weaknesses, and triggers. They recognize how their emotions can impact their decision-making and interactions with others. Being attuned to their feelings, they can better regulate their responses, especially in challenging situations. This self-control allows leaders to approach conflicts or setbacks with a calm and rational mindset, fostering an environment of resilience and adaptability within the team.

Moreover, leaders with emotional intelligence can skillfully navigate interpersonal dynamics. They possess the ability to understand and manage the emotions of others, fostering open lines of communication and effective collaboration. These leaders recognize that everyone has unique perspectives, experiences, and feelings.

Acknowledging and validating these differences creates an inclusive environment where diverse voices are respected and valued. This inclusive approach leads to enhanced creativity, innovation, and problem-solving as team members feel empowered to contribute their unique insights.

Beyond the immediate benefits of emotional intelligence, leaders who prioritize empathy and compassion also create a sense of camaraderie and support within their teams. Employees who feel their leaders genuinely care about their well-being are likelier to be engaged, motivated, and loyal to the organization. A leader's ability to demonstrate empathy and understanding during challenging times can significantly impact employee morale and resilience. Leaders promote a culture of collaboration and collective success by fostering a positive work environment where individuals feel supported.

Adapting to Change:

The rapid advancements in technology and the increasing interconnectedness brought about by globalization have completely transformed the business landscape. In this new era, effective leadership is no longer just about maintaining the status quo; it's about embracing change as an opportunity for growth and staying one step ahead of the curve.

Modern leaders understand that the ability to adapt to change is not just a desirable trait but a necessity. They recognize that clinging to outdated strategies and resisting innovation can lead to stagnation and irrelevance. Instead, they proactively seek ways to navigate uncertainty and capitalize on emerging opportunities.

Adaptable leaders possess the agility and flexibility to adjust their course when faced with unexpected challenges. They understand that change is not always linear or predictable and are prepared to pivot their strategies when necessary. These leaders are unafraid to challenge the status quo and explore new possibilities. They inspire their teams to think outside the box, encouraging them to bring forward fresh ideas and embrace innovation.

One key aspect of adapting to change is fostering a culture that encourages experimentation and learning from failure. Modern leaders understand that failures and setbacks are not roadblocks but stepping stones to success. They create an environment where taking calculated risks is celebrated, and mistakes are viewed as valuable learning experiences. By embracing a growth mindset, leaders inspire their teams to push boundaries, try new approaches, and continuously improve.

Moreover, adaptable leaders recognize that external factors do not solely drive change but can also arise within the organization. They proactively seek feedback from their team members, stakeholders, and customers, valuing diverse perspectives and staying attuned to evolving needs. They encourage open communication and collaboration, allowing ideas to flow freely throughout the organization. By fostering a culture of inclusivity and shared decision-making, these leaders tap into the collective intelligence of their teams, enabling them to adapt and respond effectively to change.

In addition to embracing change, modern leaders also play a critical role in helping their teams navigate transitions. They provide support, guidance, and reassurance during periods of uncertainty. By fostering a sense of psychological safety, they encourage their team members to embrace change, take risks, and voice their concerns or ideas without fear of judgment. These leaders understand that successful adaptation to change is a collective effort, and they actively involve their teams in the decision-making process, making them feel invested and valued.

Purpose and Meaning:

Modern leaders recognize the significance of infusing purpose and meaning into our work. They understand that when individuals find personal fulfillment and purpose in their daily tasks, they become more engaged, motivated, and committed to achieving extraordinary results.

To create a sense of purpose, modern leaders begin by aligning their organization's values with the personal values of their team members. They realize that individuals are driven by more than a paycheck; they seek a deeper connection to their work. By cultivating a workplace culture that values integrity, collaboration, and social responsibility, leaders set the stage for employees to connect their values with the organization's mission.

However, purpose cannot simply be dictated or imposed. It must be nurtured through open and authentic communication. Modern leaders effectively communicate a compelling vision that resonates with the hearts and minds of their team members. They paint a vivid picture of a future that is not solely focused on profit margins but emphasizes the positive impact their work can have on the world. By sharing stories, illustrating the organization's meaningful contributions to society, and highlighting each individual's value, leaders inspire a shared sense of purpose and ignite passion within their teams.

Moreover, purpose-driven leaders emphasize the connection between individual tasks and the organization's larger purpose. They help employees understand how their specific roles contribute to the overall mission, illustrating the importance of their contributions. Whether designing a product that improves people's lives or providing a service that brings joy to customers, leaders show how each person's work directly impacts the lives of others. This connection fosters a deep sense of fulfillment and satisfaction, transforming drudgery into a meaningful journey rather than a mundane obligation.

Modern leaders also encourage personal growth and development in cultivating purpose and meaning. They provide opportunities for individuals to pursue their passions, acquire new skills, and expand their horizons. By investing in their employees' professional and personal growth, leaders demonstrate their commitment to their team members' well-being and long-term success. This investment strengthens the organization and enables individuals to find purpose within their personal and professional journeys.

Over the past two decades, leadership has undergone a profound evolution. It has shifted from a top-down, authoritative approach to a more inclusive, collaborative, and empowering style. Today's leaders understand the value of emotional intelligence, adaptability, and purpose-driven leadership. They inspire, motivate, and create environments where everyone can thrive. As we navigate an ever-changing world, let us embrace the new face of leadership and strive to become leaders who can make a positive and lasting impact on the lives of those we lead.

Critical Factors for Evolution in Leadership:

One notable effect of technology on leadership is the demand for digital literacy. As leaders, we must easily navigate the digital landscape, leveraging technological tools and platforms to streamline processes and enhance productivity. Whether mastering project management software, harnessing the power of data analytics, or effectively utilizing social media for brand building, staying ahead in the digital era requires continuous learning and adaptation.

Moreover, technology has fostered a culture of collaboration and inclusivity. With the rise of digital platforms, leaders have been empowered to create virtual spaces encouraging participation and knowledge sharing. Remote work and virtual teams have become the norm, enabling organizations to tap into a global talent pool and leverage diverse perspectives. As leaders, we now have the opportunity to foster an environment that values and harnesses the collective intelligence of our teams.

Another significant impact of technology on leadership is the acceleration of innovation. The digital age has opened up a world of possibilities, allowing leaders to experiment, iterate, and adapt at an unprecedented pace. With vast information and cutting-edge tools, leaders can identify emerging trends, anticipate market disruptions, and drive transformative change within their organizations. Technology has dismantled traditional barriers, empowering leaders to think outside the box and challenge the status quo.[29]

Social media platforms have become invaluable tools, allowing leaders to engage in real-time conversations, share insights, and provide immediate feedback. Whether it's a quick message of appreciation or a virtual town hall meeting, leaders can now connect with their employees on a personal level, fostering a sense of belonging and collaboration.

Big data's rise has also transformed how leaders make informed decisions. In the past, gathering and analyzing data was time-consuming and arduous. With the wealth of information available at their fingertips, leaders can

[29] Arians, H. (2023, April 8). The impact of technology on leadership. People Development Magazine. https://peopledevelopmentmagazine.com/2023/04/07/impact-of-technology/

leverage data analytics to gain valuable insights into their organization's performance, customer behavior, and market trends. This enables leaders to make data-driven decisions, identify growth opportunities, and adapt strategies accordingly.

Furthermore, digital tools have allowed leaders to embrace agility and adaptability. With the aid of technology, leaders can keep a finger on the pulse of their organization, rapidly responding to challenges and seizing emerging opportunities. Leaders can promote innovation, creativity, and continuous improvement by fostering a culture of agility and empowering their teams.

The power of connectivity goes beyond the boundaries of an organization. Leaders can now engage with stakeholders, including customers, partners, and the wider community, on a global scale. Social media has become a powerful platform for leaders to share their vision, values, and achievements with the world. Through authentic and transparent communication, leaders can build trust and inspire others to join their cause. The ripple effect of these connections can extend far beyond the immediate scope of the organization, creating a positive impact on a larger scale.

However, it is essential to note that while technology has brought about immense opportunities, it has also presented challenges. The rapid pace of technological advancements requires leaders to be agile and adaptable, embracing change as an integral part of their leadership journey.

As we navigate the ever-changing leadership landscape in the digital age, one thing remains constant: the importance of human connection. While technology has undoubtedly reshaped the way we lead, it should never replace the human touch. As leaders, we must strive to foster meaningful relationships, inspire our teams, and provide a sense of purpose beyond technology.

The Changing Work Environment:

One critical factor that has brought about significant change is the nature of work itself. As more employees choose to work remotely and embrace flexible schedules, it has become crucial for leaders to adapt their styles to accommodate this new reality. This shift often requires avoiding micromanagement and fostering trust-based relationships with their teams.

Gone are the days of strict nine-to-five schedules and rigid office environments. The traditional work model, characterized by employees confined to their cubicles and closely monitored by their supervisors, has given way to a more flexible and autonomous approach. The advancement of technology, such as cloud computing, video conferencing, and project management tools, has made remote work possible and highly efficient.

This changing landscape presents an exciting opportunity for leaders to rethink their management strategies and embrace a more empowering style. Instead of being overly prescriptive and monitoring every minute detail, leaders are finding success by entrusting their teams with greater autonomy and fostering a culture of trust. This approach allows employees to have a greater sense of ownership over their work and enables them to tap into their creativity and problem-solving skills.

Trust is the cornerstone of any successful relationship, and the workplace is no exception. When leaders demonstrate trust in their teams, it creates a positive and empowering environment. Employees feel valued and respected, knowing their skills and expertise are recognized and appreciated. As a result, they are more likely to be engaged, motivated, and willing to go the extra mile to achieve shared goals.

Building trust within a team starts with clear and open communication. Leaders should establish channels for regular dialogue and encourage an environment where everyone's voice is heard and respected. Listening to employees' ideas, concerns, and feedback fosters a sense of belonging and encourages collaboration.

In addition to communication, leaders can cultivate trust by providing professional growth and development opportunities. By investing in their team members' learning and skill enhancement, leaders demonstrate their commitment to their employees' success. This investment benefits the individuals and strengthens the overall capabilities of the team and organization.

Another crucial aspect of leading with trust is recognizing and celebrating achievements. Taking the time to acknowledge and appreciate the hard work and accomplishments of individuals and the team goes a long way in building trust and fostering a positive work culture. Genuine recognition and praise boost morale and inspire employees to continue striving for excellence.

As leaders adapt to the changing nature of work, it's essential to remember that trust is not built overnight. It requires consistent effort, transparency, and a genuine belief in the capabilities of one's team. Embracing a trust-based leadership approach may initially feel uncomfortable for some, especially those accustomed to a more traditional management style. However, the benefits of cultivating trust are well worth the effort.

In this ever-evolving world of work, where employees seek greater flexibility and autonomy, leaders who embrace trust will empower their teams to thrive. By fostering an environment of trust, leaders can unlock the full potential of their employees and create a culture that inspires innovation, collaboration, and success.

Chapter 5:

The Post-COVID Era

When the global pandemic of 2020-21 COVID-19 hit planet Earth, it profoundly impacted leadership, accelerating many of the trends already in motion. With so many people working from home, leaders have had to find new ways to keep their teams motivated and engaged. This often meant focusing more on empathy, communication, and emotional intelligence than traditional command-and-control tactics.

That being said, it is imperative to discuss the impact of the COVID-19 pandemic on management and leadership. It will also discuss how it will likely shape the future of management and leadership. The post-COVID era is likely to see remote work become more prevalent, with companies needing to adopt new management and leadership practices to manage remote teams effectively. Companies must prioritize agility, resilience, and employee well-being to ensure business success.

Most times, we see that leaders prefer to have a physical presence in front of their staff. They want to lead by example, and the way it can be done is by being in front of their teams and showing them how it is done and having them follow in their footsteps. In times of pandemics, it would be hard to be in front of teams and lead by example when "social distancing" is advised.

However, modern technology has made things easier and more accessible for teams globally by means of a virtual office. Every team member is "working from home," may that " home" be a coffee shop, park, or home office. They are all connected via Zoom, Microsoft Teams, Slack, or any communication tool designed to create an effective workflow between them. Other tools include Trello, Asana, or other task management software that can work on either agile or non-agile models.

This is where the leader comes in. He can create different groups within Microsoft Teams or Slack and can delegate tasks through those means. Slack groups are known as channels and are highly effective for team communication. It works great for cross-functional teams too. Leadership will be virtual, but responsibilities and tasks will be delegated with set deadlines. We had to experience that with the COVID-19 pandemic. It literally forced us to change the way we work and live our lives, and that brings me to discuss what became known as "The New Normal."

The New Normal:

The new normal was a term given to the time when people were forced to stay in their homes and practice social adjusting. It took some getting used to, and eventually, people got adjusted to this new normal. However, now that the pandemic is over, the new normal has become the old normal. People have returned to offices or work in hybrid setups. A hybrid setup is when teams switch between the physical and home office. It is perhaps the way for the future, but it all depends on how the teams function. This is where leadership comes in, and the right leader knows how to lead his teams in a hybrid setup.

Sometimes, "work from home" setups may require micromanagement, but good employees know when to deliver on time from whatever they call home. The point is that expectations should be set, and the leader can check on each employee a few times a day to ensure timely deliveries. Virtual team structures can be hard to manage, but when a structure is properly set up, things do fall into place. However, the real challenge comes in crisis situations.

According to research, "Crises are situations that occur unexpectedly and are not a normal part of a leader's scope. These situations can be uncertain and complicated and are often dynamic in nature. Their characteristics include fragmented and often conflicting information (Sadiq et al., 2020). Leaders need to be able to quickly gain an understanding of the situation and be able to anticipate and gauge risk, gather relevant information quickly, and be able to formulate an effective response (Boin et al., 2010; Comfort et al., 2020). They need the capacity to take charge in these types of circumstances; otherwise, the situation can escalate, rendering it insurmountable (Sadiq et al., 2020). Leadership in a crisis also involves contingency planning to enact an effective response, mitigate the amount of possible damage caused, and lay the groundwork for recovery (Kapucu and Van Wart, 2008)."[30]

The above clearly explains the fundamental job of a leader. A leader has to step up his or her game in a crisis situation and steer his team out of a tricky situation. It is what Ultra Magnus, Rodimus, and Optimus Prime exactly referred to when they said, "to light our darkest hour." A

[30] AlMazrouei H. (2023). The effect of COVID-19 on managerial leadership style within Australian public sector organizations. *Journal of General Management*, 03063070231152976. https://doi.org/10.1177/03063070231152976

strong leader becomes that light in the team's darkest hour. He or she leads them with a "never say die" attitude. This can be evident when working virtually.

If this means, leaders should get their teams together for a virtual Zoom call huddle and devise a strategy. Strategies can be developed through discussions with team members. The idea is also never to create panic. Leaders cannot lead when there is panic among team members, and jobs are at risk. If you remember, several people globally lost their jobs because some industries got impacted, such as tourism and live entertainment. Cineplexes and multiplexes faced closure due to the lack of people visiting the theaters. Therefore, job security was a massive concern for pandemic workers. Companies began shrinking their workforce to save costs, and layoffs occurred as a result. An effective leader and manager can get the best out of his or her team in a pandemic situation. That leader can retain the entire team and make them work hard and smart to ensure a regular revenue stream.

As per research from AlMazrouei, H. (2023), "The devolution of responsibility for the management of certain facets of responsibility in more stable times does much to engender a culture of trust and cooperation. This culture will help to formulate a better, more effective response to any crisis situations that occur (Kezar et al., 2018), as it allows better quality decision-making to occur, derived through a combination of various viewpoints (Kezar and Holcombe, 2017). Once this culture is established, the leader can plan and coordinate their response to any crisis, secure in the knowledge that their team members will provide trustworthy advice and effective cooperation (Fernandez and Shaw, 2020)."

It is very accurate that leadership and management get tested a lot during pandemics because one needs to know crisis management. A pandemic already represents a crisis situation, so it is wise not to cause any commotion, stress, and anxiety among team members. This is where leaders must keep things cool and ensure that their teams' jobs are safe, and together they can pull through this.

Pandemic Leadership Styles:

Leadership styles can vary, and one can use the different styles discussed in previous chapters. The key word here is "effectiveness." Leadership effectiveness was initially attributed to leaders' personality traits. Personality here has been looked at in regards to stable tendencies and cannot be modified. On the other hand, the behavioral outlook on leadership describes it as a behavioral style. This suggests that leadership can be taught, and individuals could receive training to become effective leaders. This also invokes the fact that leadership skills comprise a mix of communication, behavioral and cognitive skills.

These skills demand various learning experiences. It is further observed that situational leadership pushes the idea that effective leadership is a solid mix between a specific leadership style and situation. We can infer that a leadership style becomes effective in a certain case while another style would suit another situation.

Transformational and charismatic leadership has received a lot of attention in the last few decades. It is observed that transformational leaders encourage their followers by increasing involvement and performance. They give guidance and critical feedback, are respectful of their colleague's needs, and help them to become more innovative and creative. Furthermore, they stimulate their followers to accomplishments by going beyond their expectations. This required a transformation of beliefs, attitudes, and values. This caused increased performance.

As per Fiedler's Leadership Contingency Model (Fiedler, 1989, 2005), leadership effectiveness is dependent on the situation and contingencies. He described the situations as based upon three dimensions (AlMazrouei, H., 2023), as follows:

- Task structure

- The leader-follower interpersonal relationship

- The leader's level of authority over the follower

- Contingency leadership has received less attention, particularly in regard to the COVID-19 pandemic. Fieldler's model explains the idea of two specific kinds of leaders:

- Task-oriented leaders

- Relationship-oriented leaders

Each kind of leader is effective in particular situations. Cognitive Resource Theory (CRT) (Murphy et al., 1992) furthered Fiedler's model with additional traits to the original contingency leadership model (Fiedler, 1989) by focusing on leadership's stress response. CRT outlines conditions where leaders and followers will more likely utilize their intelligence, knowledge, and skills to alleviate behavioral stress consequences. Fiedler's model proclaims a directly proportional relationship between experience and intelligence, to performance. This means there is an increase in performance levels among highly intelligent and experienced leaders. Experience counts a lot because leaders can draw on their plethora of experience to guide their teams in specific situations. Emotional intelligence comes in handy. Therefore, intelligent and experienced leadership is the way to go, especially in pandemic situations.

Talking Points:

We have discussed the different leadership styles and theories that effectively work in a pandemic situation. We also described how things massively change in these situations with social distancing and virtual offices. There was discussion on the move toward a hybrid leadership model and its challenges. Leaders face stress but cannot pass it on to their followers and team members. It takes the right mettle to get teams to work in pandemic situations by avoiding panic and ensuring job security. Hopefully, leaders can take positive points from the discussed leadership models and apply them in future pandemic situations.

Chapter 6:

Effectiveness of Emotional Intelligence

EI (Emotional Intelligence) is crucial in effective decision-making, communication, and relationship building in leadership and management. Leaders and managers with high EI are better equipped to manage stress, inspire and motivate their team members, and build a positive work environment.

Developing emotional intelligence is essential for leaders and managers to achieve success in their roles. Some ways to establish EI include self-reflection, active listening, practicing empathy, and seeking feedback from others. By focusing on these skills, leaders and managers can improve their emotional awareness, regulate their emotions, and develop stronger relationships with their team members.

Emotional intelligence can lead to successful outcomes when applied in leadership and management. This type of leadership can increase team morale, improve productivity, and lead to a more positive work environment.

We previously understood how emotional intelligence has emerged as a foundation of effective leadership. It has redefined how leaders interact with their teams and nurture a more positive and productive work environment. In the past, the traditional image of a leader was often associated with toughness and emotional detachment. However, the evolving leadership landscape has emphasized the significance of empathy, self-awareness, and understanding and managing emotions.[31]

Leaders with high emotional intelligence possess a remarkable capacity to connect with others on a deeper level. They are genuinely interested in their team members' thoughts, feelings, and concerns. By listening actively and empathizing with their employees, these leaders create an atmosphere of trust and psychological safety. When individuals feel seen and heard, they are more likely to express their ideas, share their concerns, and contribute to the team's success.

As you will read later in this chapter, self-awareness is another vital aspect of emotional intelligence in leadership.

---

[31] Landry, L. (2019, April 3). Emotional intelligence in leadership: Why it's important. Business Insights Blog.
https://online.hbs.edu/blog/post/emotional-intelligence-in-leadership

Leaders who clearly possess self-awareness understand their strengths, weaknesses, and triggers. They recognize how their emotions can impact their decision-making and interactions with others. Being attuned to their feelings, they can better regulate their responses, especially in challenging situations. This self-control allows leaders to approach conflicts or setbacks with a calm and rational mindset, fostering an environment of resilience and adaptability within the team.

Furthermore, leaders with emotional intelligence can skillfully navigate interpersonal dynamics. They possess the ability to understand and manage the emotions of others, fostering open lines of communication and effective collaboration. These leaders recognize that everyone has unique perspectives, experiences, and feelings. Acknowledging and validating these differences creates an inclusive environment where diverse voices are respected and valued. This inclusive approach leads to enhanced creativity, innovation, and problem-solving as team members feel empowered to contribute their unique insights.

Beyond the immediate benefits of emotional intelligence, leaders who prioritize empathy and compassion also create a sense of camaraderie and support within their teams. Employees who feel their leaders genuinely care about their well-being are likelier to be engaged, motivated, and loyal to the organization. A leader's ability to demonstrate empathy and understanding during challenging times can significantly impact employee morale and resilience. Leaders promote a culture of collaboration and collective success by fostering a positive work environment where individuals feel supported.

The Significance of Emotional Intelligence in Leadership:

In the modern business world, it is essential to have both soft and technical skills. If you want to grow into a leadership role, technical skills assist in moving into a management position. At the same time, soft skills assist in bringing solid leadership traits into your repertoire and nurturing encouraging workplace relationships.

Emotional intelligence is a crucial leadership skill that mainly equips you with the necessary skills to mentor team members efficiently, fix concerns, and initiate collaboration with colleagues. We have understood how emotional effectiveness works with leaders, but we will now delve deeper into its essence.

Emotional Intelligence 101:

As we have understood already, emotional intelligence applies to an individual's ability to realize, assess, and handle his or her emotions. It also reflects on your management of emotions during interaction with others. Developing emotional intelligence enables improvement in workplace relationships and most certainly rubs off well on team members and peers.

An increased level of emotional intelligence translates into understanding and realizing your feelings. It allows you to understand their meaning and impact on others. Leaders with high emotional intelligence can best manage their emotions to cause favorable results accurately.

This is a must-have skill for leaders. It helps them effectively manage teams without causing rifts or conflicts. Emotionally intelligent leaders are able to get the most out of their employees and adapt their leadership style as needed to accommodate employees with different personalities.

The Fantastic Five: The Five Pillars of Emotional Intelligence

Emotional Intelligence usually consists of five critical areas:

- Self-awareness
- Self-regulation
- Social awareness
- Social skills

- Self-motivation

Managers are encouraged to work on the above areas and step up their game to become highly emotionally intelligent business leaders.

Self-Awareness

Being aware of your feelings before being aware of others is essential. You can get the most out of yourself, and leaders are required to do that to be the best of the best. Your feelings can impact the feelings of your team members, so you have to be smart enough to express your feeling so they do not rub them the wrong way. Self-awareness allows any leader to understand his or her emotions, weaknesses, and strengths.

Self-Regulation

Self-regulation is also known as self-management, and it denotes an individual's willingness to control and manage emotions. It is critical for leaders to keep their emotions in check and stay positive in front of their team despite the level of challenges they are facing. Team members look up to you for inspiration and guidance, so you must show that nervy leadership. Nerves of steel set leaders apart from the rest. Challenges are part and parcel of everyday business life, so leaders must show bravery and calm in tough times.

Social Awareness

Social awareness and empathy go hand-in-hand because you have to understand how others feel and emote. Team communications highly depend on leaders' level of understanding of team members' feelings and emotions. Empathetic leadership is designed to be supportive of their professional and personal growth. Furthermore, empathetic leaders go out of their way to efficiently manage positive workplace self-esteem.

Social Skills

Successful leadership is dependent on social skills. These include the ways you navigate daily tasks, delegation of work, communicate, guide, mentor, collaborate, and influence team members. Furthermore, it even includes how you deal with conflict management and challenges. If you have developed social skills to the point that you can manage a positive workplace environment and atmosphere, it comes back to you in dividends and benefits the entire team.

Self-Motivation

Effective managers must be well-adapted to self-motivation because they should not be afraid to face challenges. They have to keep reminding them that they can meet any challenge with a "you can do it" attitude and that no task is too big or too small. No challenge is tough enough to accomplish. Leaders have their professional and personal goals to accomplish, and therefore, they must work toward those milestones, including organizational goals. Self-motivation in employees is the tool of the leadership trade, and every leader must hold themselves to a higher standard of efficiency and productivity.

Now that we are aware of the five emotional intelligence pillars, we must understand their real benefits for leaders and employees. Emotional intelligence is clearly a key component of business leadership. A lack of it can cause the following:

- Negative performance
- Negative productivity
- Absenteeism

The terrible three above can result in culture breakdown and horribly impact the bottom line. Therefore, the following six emotional intelligence benefits are as follows:

Improved Teamwork:

Highly emotionally intelligent employees are better team players due to several reasons. They have better communication skills and are more open to idea sharing, and are actively good listeners. They are not control freaks because they care about the rest of the team. Such employees place a high value on coworker input and ideas due to the increased trust between them. Teamwork of the highest regard is displayed by showing thoughtfulness, respect, and consideration, and employers value that. It also helps them become highly influential and effective leaders.

Improved Workplace Atmosphere:

An emotionally intelligent workforce lower overall stress and increase self-esteem in the company. Furthermore, a culture nurturing mutual respect, compassion, and friendliness is considered a very powerful one. Therefore, employees are more inclined to come to work every single day and abstain from absenteeism because they enjoy the work culture. A workplace that treats employees like family is a sign of emotionally intelligent leadership.

Quick Adaptability:

"Adapt and persevere" is the mantra of the modern 21st-century workplace. Businesses should avoid stagnation, and therefore a change is always a good thing. In fact, change is the only constant in life, so companies must change with the times. Just see how Amazon and Netflix have succeeded. They adopted current trends while still keeping classic offerings because of their growing customer base.

For many years until this later this year, Netflix was still rending out DVDs and Blu-rays as part of DVD.com while growing their streaming offerings which has now become their primary business. They were able to appeal to all customers' preferences. Amazon has continued to add services and copy Netflix to a larger extent by having in-house studios, original shows, and more. They even offered groceries. This is because their leadership tapped into their customers' emotions and delivered.

That being said, companies tend to change more when their employees are consistently striving for self-improvement and grow the company at the same time. These employees are well-aware that organizational changes and even drastic ones like restructuring and rightsizing are not favored by all of them even though they could be the best for the company.

Highly emotionally intelligent employees are able to adjust easily and endorse a change to grow with the company. Such an exciting attitude rubs off very well on other peers and creates a highly positive workplace atmosphere.

Higher Self-Awareness:

Emotionally intelligent individuals are well aware of their weaknesses and strengths. They are open to constructive feedback to achieve personal and professional growth. Managers are familiar with individuals who are not keen to listen to constructive criticism, which eventually results in frustration and hinders productivity. Furthermore, there are times when employees find it challenging to realize their limitations.

Highly emotionally intelligent individuals have increased self-awareness and can better judge what they can accomplish in a set time. On the other hand, other individuals over-commit and under-deliver because they do not know what they are capable of accomplishing.

Greater Self-Control:

Emotionally intelligent individuals are fine-tuned to manage challenging circumstances. It could be many challenges, like dealing with a manager who despises your work quality or an unhappy client. All these situations warrant calm and avoidance of emotional anger outcries.

Such individuals are aware that any irrational or negative behavior will only escalate matters to a never-ending series of events. It will be akin to running around in circles for no reason whatsoever. These individuals are well-versed in practicing restraint and displaying controlled emotions as per the presented circumstance.

Always Being a Step Ahead:

While emotional intelligence is valued very highly in the workplace, not all companies understand its significance. This has hence resulted in teams that feel undervalued or completely not at all. Competition thrives when emotionally intelligent individuals lead companies, and those same leaders hire emotionally intelligent talent. An excellent way to inculcate emotional intelligence is to include EQ training in the employee wellness program.

One of the best ways to foster emotional intelligence is to focus on each individual in the team. This provides the business a competitive advantage over its rivals and leaves them bedazzled by how their teams lack compassion and teamwork and are demotivated.

The benefits of EI are pretty apparent, and it is a wise decision to analyze the existing workforce in your business and pick out those who are high on emotional intelligence. These would be the perfect candidates for leadership and management positions, so it would not hurt to give them a chance and perhaps increase their motivation to work harder, smarter, and grow with the company. While it would be hard to argue not to choose an experienced individual for leadership and management roles, the employee displaying high levels of EI would be a much more worthy choice. A candidate displaying both would be even better because he or she would have the best of both worlds because they could rely on their experiences where they showed high EI.

It would be best to upgrade the interview process by incorporating questions that encourage candidates to display emotional intelligence, other than the standard experience, education, qualifications, and technical background questions. You would be surprised how the candidates answer those questions and make the hiring process rather easier for you. This is one excellent way to build a highly capable and emotionally intelligent team pretty quickly.

As you have seen, emotional intelligence is highly contagious and catches on, and it starts right from the top management to the bottom. The top management will inspire others and ensures that every employee on their payroll is emotionally intelligent because they will work and grow with the company and will adapt to any given situation. Emotional intelligence is a critical trait in today's workplace, and those who can apply it in their daily lives at home and at work are bound to succeed in all facets of life.

Chapter 7:

Importance of Culture and Diversity

E ffective leadership and management require a deep understanding and appreciation of culture and diversity in today's globalized world. Influential leaders recognize the importance of diversity and can leverage it to create a more inclusive and innovative workplace.

One of the key benefits of a diverse workforce is the ability to bring different perspectives and ideas to the table. Leaders who value diversity and inclusivity are more likely to foster collaboration and creativity. Leaders who understand and respect the culture of their employees are more likely to create a positive work environment and foster a sense of belonging.

However, it is essential to note that culture and diversity are not just about being politically correct. Leaders who fail to value diversity and understand cultural norms and practices risk alienating employees and missing out on valuable opportunities. Effective leaders recognize the importance of creating an inclusive culture where everyone feels valued and respected.

Diversity has become a norm as the world has become smaller. If you go down the credits reel of any major motion picture these days, you will see a diverse list of names, and you can tell these individuals hail from various parts of the world. In the United States, you will see various races and ethnicities in offices, and this is incredible because diversity should be celebrated. It does not matter where the individual is from or what his or her last name is, and they should be selected for work based on their qualifications, merit, and experience. There is a good reason why every American business touts itself as an "equal opportunity employer." This is because these businesses embrace and celebrate diversity.

Diversity is not just celebrated by corporations but is widely observed in academic institutions and even sports teams. In fact, if you look at European club soccer, globally renowned clubs like Liverpool, Manchester United, and Real Madrid have players from all across the world on their roster. One of Liverpool's top players, Mohammed Salah, hails from Eqypt and is widely known among his fans as

"The Egyptian King," "The Pharoah," and "Egyptian (Lionel) Messi," among others.

Diversity is beautiful because it allows organizations to choose the best individuals from any ethnicity, and these individuals can bring a lot from their culture and experiences to the table. There is an excellent global exchange of ideas and insights. It is highly recommended to have diverse leadership to take advantage of workplace diversity. If that is not the case, the local and native leadership must take advantage of the diverse workforce.

A diverse leadership can assist in establishing and developing trust with several individuals in the organization because they understand the different cultural needs. It even brings immense knowledge and distinct perspectives. Together, they can improve leadership quality by developing relationships with both internal and external stakeholders.

Another excellent benefit of diversity is how it allows individuals to have a better awareness of upcoming opportunities, manage handles without much difficulty, and make diversity-friendly decisions. Diverse leadership can go a long way in ensuring high employee retention rates, bringing in top talent, and fostering a healthy workplace culture.

It is becoming the norm to deeply evaluate the current workforce and leadership teams much differently than previously. It is no longer about ticking off a checklist of experience, education, and other qualifications. The way modern marketplace has evolved in this century and millennium to the point where companies look beyond the traditional criteria. These days, it is about measuring workplace diversity because that brings new and fresh ideas to the table and the ability to reach wider and new markets that have been previously untapped. These days, it is even more essertial to have a very diverse leadership.

Every manager is different, but those who step out of the crowd are the ones that have some vital traits that turn them into excellent leaders. Those traits include skillful communication, critical thinking, problem-solving, and decisiveness. These all translate into effective and capable leadership no matter the size of the team or diversity level. The higher the diversity, that is better, but those who embrace it will be able to build a diverse team.

Textbooks and business school classes can only teach you so much, and some of the above skills can be absorbed, understood, and incorporated. Still, nothing beats real-world experience and natural abilities. In fact, it may be rather challenging to develop diversity-friendly leadership traits, but that adoption can become much better with highly diverse leadership teams.

Defining Workplace Diversity:

There has already been enough discussion and examples of workplace diversity in this chapter, but we have yet to hammer down a definitive definition of diversity and, most importantly, leadership diversity. A solid definition of diversity is incorporating individuals in a company from various backgrounds, and that is seen throughout the workforce.

Categories must also be defined, and those include race, ethnicity, gender, and age as the primary factors. However, more categories have been added under the diversity umbrella, like economic background, political alliance, religion/ faith tradition, disability status, and sexual orientation, among others.

When we define diversity, it is not about how individuals identify as. It also is incumbent on the business to be accepting of diversity and coexistence. The business must support people who may be different, but they promote such individuals' voices. An inclusive work environment is part and parcel of a diversity-friendly workplace culture regardless of leadership or non-leadership roles, including mid and entry-level positions.

Although we have accomplished significant diversity in many companies, there is still a long way to go. Research from Fortune magazine in 2020 states that 37 companies, including four Fortune 500 companies, are managed by Black and female CEOs, correspondingly (*Importance of Diversity in Leadership | Maryville Online*, 2021).[32]

The percentage breakdown of every management position assigned to diverse professionals as per the U.S. Bureau of Labor Statistics (BLS) is as follows:

- Women: 40%
- Hispanic: 11%
- Black: 8%
- Asian: 6%

(*Importance of Diversity in Leadership | Maryville Online*, 2021)

Benefits of Leadership Diversity:

Leadership diversity has several benefits, but not all of them can be measured or physically shown. However, they are still pretty impactful on the business that is managed by diverse leaders. The following benefits are some of the best that any company can take advantage of, and that is leadership diversity-friendly. For the most part, we see

---

[32] *Importance of Diversity in Leadership | Maryville Online*. (2021, February 4). Maryville Online.
https://online.maryville.edu/blog/diversity-in-leadership/

improvement in processes and a pretty strong corporate profile. It even includes brownie points from the wider community and all stakeholders.

Pioneering Thinking:

Leadership diversity usually translates into thought diversity. You will encounter a massive difference when you see multiple diverse individuals, in terms of background, in idea development that covers a vast field. This phenomenon would be unseen when you have a single category management team in terms of age, race, background, or demographic.

Diverse leadership allows you to pull from a wider range of thoughts with access to various personal and cultural experiences. This is what is pretty much known as "out-of-the-box thinking." A company employing diverse leadership and workforce can successfully employ this thinking.

Broader Skill Sets Range:

You can teach some skills to others, but some just come naturally to them. Diverse management teams bring a whole lot to the table, and that range from backgrounds, skills, characteristics, traits, and knowledge. Google may never be as successful today had it not been managed by diverse leadership. Sundar Pichai, its CEO, hails from an

Indian background. Microsoft CEO Satya Nadella also has Indian roots. It is natural to see the younger workforce be more in tune with modern technology and social media. Companies wanting to be more social media-friendly can hire younger employees that know how to make the best of social media and are perhaps influencers themselves. The older generation may be averse to social media, so they may not be able to bring too much or zero traction via social media to the business.

Progressive Company Culture:

Leadership diversity nurtures more close relationships with employees. There is a much wider family feeling at the workplace and the management. It goes to show that leadership cares about employees. Employees see their own backgrounds and cultures represented at all levels of the corporate hierarchy, so they know that they can reach someone from their background easily because of the high levels of accessibility. This goes a long way to show that management is very diversity-friendly, believes in coexistence, and allows junior employees to move up the corporate ladder in the company. Inclusivity is essential and increases employee retention rates tenfold because employees feel very comfortable where they are because they feel respected there at the end of the day. This brings in more employees from diverse backgrounds through good word-of-mouth.

Stronger Company Profile:

A company's values are reflected by its management. It gives them a lot of positive press and goodwill when companies stress diversity at all corporate levels, especially in management positions. It gives the public the impression that such companies value different cultures, ideas, and inclusivity. They can cater to a broader target audience and tap into new markets, especially when expanding globally. The best companies in the world that operate globally realize the significance of internal diversity and how it benefits businesses in different countries and especially those places where the culture is radically different from the one at home. Employees prefer seeing their representation in management, and unsurprisingly also goes the same for customers. Diversity allows companies to be connected globally, bringing more opportunities to expand and succeed to the table.

Final Words: Embrace Diversity!

Diversity is clearly valued in the global business landscape, so many companies should join the bandwagon and celebrate and embrace it more than ever. It makes a massive difference in today's super-connected world, and all stakeholders appreciate these movies.

Such corporations are globally relevant, and you have seen how that has made a difference to Google and Microsoft. PepsiCo once had an Indian female CEO Indra Nooyi, and that definitely put Pepsi higher on the diversity scale because they nailed on two areas: having a female CEO and that too from India. This was a massive accomplishment for India and women, so such measures should be encouraged in other companies too.

Therefore, it is imperative for all corporations to embrace and celebrate diversity if they want to go global and tap untapped markets and also move up in their home countries.

Chapter 8:

Impact of Technology

In this chapter, we have explored the impact of technology on effective leadership and management. It highlights that technology is a tool that can improve communication, efficiency, productivity, and decision-making. Furthermore, it can help leaders engage with their teams and foster a sense of belonging, resulting in improved employee engagement and performance. However, ethical implications, such as data privacy and security, should also be considered. The conclusion emphasizes that technology should be utilized as a tool, not a substitute, for effective leadership and management. Leaders who understand the impact of technology can leverage it to enhance their effectiveness and achieve their objectives.

Here is one rule of thumb when it concerns technology and management, never make technology a substitute for any person or role, but make it your best friend. It can genuinely complement exemplary leadership if used in the correct manner. These days, we have to rely on technology to optimize and automate processes to cut down on costs and labor resources and ensure that the savings pass on to the customers.

Technology can act as a powerful asset for high-level management. It allows for highly effective leadership to take place. When we talk about highly effective management, it encompasses several traits, including diversity, communication, learning, and change. Technology's impact stimulates a brand-new leadership style. It is more in line with modern sensibilities and thinking because the markets have changed and adapted to the new technology, and if you do not, you will lag behind. This is why you always have to stay ahead of the game and keep adapting your leadership style to stay in line with the times.

Adapt and Persevere:

Leadership development execution and planning are impacted by technology and digital disruption shifts. You will see how the workforce has changed, and technology has developed to influence a different leadership and working style. It can create new industries and eliminate some old ones. For example, the printing press is on life support as digital media has all but taken over entirely in all forms of information and entertainment media. We saw how video rental stores have pretty much disappeared, and the most significant example of that is Blockbuster Video. There is just one store open now in Bend, Oregon. Blockbuster once had the opportunity to purchase Netflix but decided against it. Netflix founder Jeff Hastings must be laughing now at their mistake. Netflix kept its DVD rental business while focusing on emerging streaming technologies and is now one of the most prominent players in commercial video streaming.

Let's take the example of Redbox. The Redbox kiosks are in all major supermarkets and chain stores where you could choose a DVD or Blu-ray movie to rent for just a dollar a night. This is an evolution of the traditional Blockbuster video rental formula, and Redbox has pretty much survived in the face of streaming. Here is the thing that pretty much matters. The conclusion of these factors is the reason why new skills and strategies are required to meet market requirements. This necessitates the existence of well-trained leaders. As seen in the case of Blockbuster, completely developed leadership proficiencies are necessary to meet current and constantly changing market demands. Organizations will then suffer market decline or share.

Therefore, businesses have endorsed the requirement of organized leadership development training and experiences alongside career and leadership development programs. Technology has been a real game changer in the industry with electronic processing, automation, high virtual teams collaboration, and improved work-life balance via remote and virtual working opportunities. We saw a taste of this when the COVID-19 pandemic hit the world, but truth be told, virtual offices have always been around since the internet developed to a point where remote work became a possibility. This is a case where technological cases do not always bring about leadership development endeavors. We will focus, however, on how technology impacts leadership and management in this chapter.

Leadership with Change:

Technology has allowed leaders to manage teams better and give them greater autonomy and freedom to work with less micromanagement. There is one thing employees dislike, and that is micromanagement. No one likes a manager who is constantly hovering over their shoulders like a hawk. Employees prefer working for businesses that allow them flexibility and fair work-life balance. This ensures less stress and anxiety at the workplace and boosts productivity. Leaders must provide a reasonable work-life balance because that is the key to winning their team's trust. If someone cannot work from an office at all, remote work situations can be set up so that person can work effectively from wherever convenient, but he or she must adhere to project and team deadlines. There cannot be any slacking off, procrastination, or late deliveries. Leaders must ensure that the message goes through that virtual offices do not give the team members license to slack off.

Work can be submitted digitally via task management software or emails. The agile system of working has created new rules and protocols for working in highly tech-impacted workplaces where the teams are working on current or emergent technologies. Agile translates into the skill to move easily and quickly. In business, it refers to an "anytime, any place, anywhere" mindset. This allows employees to work in an environment where they are free to work as they please as per their requirements and deliverables.

Agile Leadership:

In agile workplace environments, employees are divided into scrum teams and can be asked to work on sprints. If you are wondering what sprint entails, it basically starts off with sprint planning. The planning part is what starts the sprint. It determines the sprint deliverables and ways to accomplish those deliverables and goals. Therefore, sprint planning is done on the advice and participation of all team members. The software used for agile sprint planning includes Asana, Trello, and Jira. A lot of sprint planning work is involved in project management initiatives in high-tech software companies.

The person involved with leading the scrums is known as the scrum master or coach, and it is that person who initiates sprint planning. There are two other individuals involved, known as the product owner and the rest of the team. The way it works is that the product owner determines the contender product backlog matters and related deliverables. He or she also suggests a sprint goal. The team members then figure out which of the product backlog matters they could compete within the sprint target and how they plan to accomplish those product backlog deliverables. The scrum master or coach enables sprint planning to ensure adequate discussion and eventual sprint goal agreement from everyone involved. Furthermore, he or she determines whether the correct product backlog matters to get inclusion in the backlog.

One thing you must understand is that agile planning, framework, and leadership only work in specific fields and work environments. This is when new software features have to be deployed, and scrum masters can make use of cross-functional teams or ensure every team plays its role to launch the feature as targeted because stakeholders are made aware of the launch dates. This is where sprint planning comes in handy and is a product of modern workplaces and leadership styles, which I believe could be considered distributive. Technology plays a massive role because the teams are working in the tech space, and deadlines can be very stringent. This is the reason why spring planning is mighty effective.

The Tools of the Trade:

Technology has allowed employees to operate independently and give managers a way to supervise from far off. It pretty much allows for a virtual office to function. It will enable real-time monitoring of tasks and deliverables. It increases accountability among both leaders and teams. Leaders and managers can offer the required feedback on the processes and deliverables status wherever the team is performing.

Team communication software such as Slack, Discord, Microsoft Teams, Google Meet/ Hangouts, and Zoom are excellent options to choose from for such a virtual office to function. Success relies on the fact that managers choose to utilize technology to their advantage. The examples given here make things easier for both team members and managers to achieve corporate goals. A lot of this type of work functionality was discussed previously in the COVID-19 leadership chapter, so you could return to that and see how seamlessly a virtual office functioned. The following are ways in which effective leadership can take the workplace to a whole level with modern technology.

Flexible Working Environment:

Even though remote work and virtual offices have been around for some time, it was only until the COVID-19 pandemic that they went mainstream. Modern technology allows teams separated by state and national borders and geographic distances to work together in real time. These teams can accomplish tasks without being together in a confined office space. This method of work is slowly being considered outdated as virtual offices cut down on several costs like gas, rental and utility bills, and other overheads. Office environments worked before when such technology was not in place. These days, offices in different parts of the world can collaborate remotely thanks to modern technology tools and software. Therefore, leaders may choose to use technology to establish a collaborative work environment for any dedicated team member wanting to do the best work for the business. It also provides that team member the flexibility and ease to work from wherever he or she can be most productive.

Remote Management made Easier – Anytime and Any Place:

These days, there are tons of excellent communications tools and software thanks to modern technology. Zoom was not invented during COVID-19 but was already present. It just became popular when everyone was forced to work from home and adopt social distancing protocols. Task management software allows managers to keep tabs on all completed work in real time. This allows the better direction of the leadership skills of managers.

Managers can now seamlessly request reports for substantial decision-making from any place n the world. We have mentioned several video conferencing applications that enable such management to take place effectively. A few not mentioned earlier include Skype and Go To Meeting, which can be used to plan and confirm team meetings. Pretty much anything can be accomplished remotely and defeats the purpose of micromanagement, which is something many team members may not enjoy. Gone are the days when bosses and managers will always be looking over the shoulders of their employees and team members.

Becoming Bilingual:

These days, the world has gotten smaller with teams in several parts of the world, and managers must cross the language barrier for effective communication. Language translation and learning tools and software can help managers collaborate with team members with fundamental to intermediate fluency in their language or mother tongue. This is why it is said that a definite characteristic of authentic leadership is success via adversity. There is so much you can do with these tools, and they will make you bilingual in no time. Technology has advanced so much that the preparation and translation of work documents in any language is possible with the click of a button. It is incredible what technology can do, and it sometimes leaves you breathless.

Language is now no longer held as a communication barrier and opens ways to inclusion and diversity within the workplace. We discussed this aspect in great detail in the workplace diversity chapter, and you can return to it to get more information on this area. In short, it helps managers build solid teams with various skills, talents, experiences, and qualifications within the organization, and these could hail from all parts of the world. Technology has opened gates to conducting business in new global markets because of the ease of translation and being bilingual. You could pretty much close deals in any part of the world without encountering any language barriers.

Automated Leadership and Management:

The best part about modern and emerging technology is how it can save leaders, managers, and senior executives a ton of time due to automation. It has been seen that artificial intelligence is given plenty of importance these days. Virtual artificial intelligence (AI) technology such as voice-activated assistants, Apple's Siri, Google Assistant (hello Google!), and Amazon's Alexa will keep managers informed and abreast of all critical meetings, appointments, and telecons. They do not have to constantly check their calendars and schedules to remind themselves of these commitments. The intelligence of these assistants is unmatched and gets better with each upgrade. AI is the latest buzzword these days in the workplace, significantly where technologies and tools like ChatGPT are mentioned, which can greatly help content creators if used correctly.

Automation allows for faster task completion. This means more work can be accomplished in less time than before. Decision-making processes are now automated thanks to the use of data, artificial intelligence, and analytics in the most suitable methods. Managers can use the tools and software most convenient for them and whichever ones that allow them to get the most work done in the shortest amount of time and with as less micromanagement as possible.

As you can see, technology has impacted leadership substantially and for the greater good. There are countless advantages of technology if utilized correctly, and the best part is new tools are discovered daily. While these technological advances are excellent, there is a flip side. It presents an ever-growing challenge for leaders and managers to stay technology adept, proficient, savvy, and ahead of the curve at all times to keep an edge over their competition. If they do not, their competitors can seize the advantage. That being said, technology has empowered leaders in more ways possible than ever before.

Technology never stays constant as it is constantly evolving. It has been said that the only constant in the world is change, and that applies to technology too. Today's technology can become outdated in two years or less. What is technology if one is ever asked to define it? It covers pretty much every evolution and trend in IT solutions, electronics, and advanced computing and extends to social leadership concepts and social media.

Modern leaders can take massive advantage of a vast array of communication challenges to get their inspirational messages to employees and team members. Managers can double as influencers to drive sales teams to deliver their best, nurture customer loyalty, and establish connections with peers via the growing amounts of social media blogs and platforms. Managers should naturally switch to coaches, guides, and mentors to their teams as the need arises, and technology can allow them to wear several hats and switch them as required naturally.

Therefore, we can conclude that technology plays a crucial part in modern leadership and can change the game for any manager who wants to stay ahead of the curve.

Chapter 9:

Ethics and Values

As we move to chapter nine, we start by understanding ethics and values and their relevance to leadership and management. Ethics can be defined as the principles that govern our behavior and decision-making, while values refer to the beliefs and attitudes that guide our actions. Leaders prioritizing ethics and values create an organizational culture of accountability, transparency, and integrity.

Furthermore, we will also be looking at and analyzing the relationship between ethics, values, and organizational success. In addition, the chapter will highlight some key ethical considerations that leaders and managers should consider. Finally, the chapter will provide practical tips for leaders and managers who want to incorporate ethics and values into their management style. This could include creating a code of conduct for employees, providing ethics training, and creating an open-door policy where employees feel comfortable raising concerns about unethical behavior.

The Balance of Power:

You must have heard the saying if you were ever a Spider-Man fan, "With great power comes great responsibility." These were the last golden words Uncle Ben told Peter Parker, and those words became his mantra for his superhero career as the web-slinger, and now we must add one more line to this mantra. With great responsibility comes great power. As you can see, there needs to be a fair balance between power and responsibility. When that balance is upset, problems happen. Unfortunately, that is the way of life of any leader when they are unable to keep things in control and let ethics and morals get out of the way. Leadership comes with a lot of things, including honesty, integrity, and accountability. In fact, I would like to echo former Olympic gold medalist and WWE professional wrestler Kurt Angle when he mentioned his "three Is." Those included integrity, intensity, and intelligence. If you go back a few chapters, you will read about emotional intelligence (EQ), and you can see where intelligence plays a role in that. Intensity is ingrained in leaders because they are ready for any challenge. Integrity means doing your work or leading with honor.

Ethics and Leadership Values:

What is it about ethics and values in leadership that is so important? It is essential that we all understand this as leaders or soon-to-be-leaders. If you lead with honor and integrity, your team members will respect you. That respect goes a long way because you do not want to come across as a fascist or slave driver. You want to ensure that your team achieves proper work-life balance. When we work in business, managers need to ensure transparency, accountability, and constant feedback provision to team members. They also must follow the leader's example if he or she leads by example. You must inspire, guide, and mentor your team members. You need to nurture their personal and professional growth. It would be best if you instilled a sense of responsibility in them so they can be better leaders when they attain management positions.

There are two perspectives on ethical leadership. The first one is collective, which means influencing team members to practice ethical behavior. This is done via leadership by example. You set a direction for that behavior and have others observe and act upon it. Therefore, ethical leaders are positive influences on their team members and offer action sets and ways to adopt those actions for everyone's mutual benefit.

The other perspective is personal and ethical leadership gives the manager reputation and credibility. It establishes authority and allows the manager to command respect instead of demanding it. It is a long road to establish that authority and respect. Unethical behavior can move the leader automatically out of the top and put the business's brand and reputation in question. Furthermore, it also hinders the self-confidence of any manager and makes things challenging for that leader to express one's complete potential.

Code of Conduct:

When it comes to creating a code of conduct, it should be made in consultation with the human resources department and devised as per company policy. It should be communicated to everyone, and the entire team and leadership must be held accountable for it. If you do not follow the rules, you do not belong in the business. That is a rule of thumb.

Ethics Training:

This brings us to ethics training. How can this be accomplished? We can introduce an ethics book for all employees or have workshops that explain common workplace ethics. Organizations specializing in such workshops can help teams achieve the tasks and explain common sense and ethics so every employee stays in line. These workshops can create a learning culture and can be held multiple times a year to foster the idea of ethical leadership and working in the office space.

Open-door Policy:

So, what does an open-door policy mean? It means employees are allowed to speak to managers freely and discuss their concerns regarding workplace ethics issues. It should be a safe space to talk so that the problems are heard and acted on. If there is an allegation against another employee by the concerned employee, a thorough investigation must take place. A decision and penalty can be awarded to the guilty party, and the policy of "innocent until proven guilty" must prevail. The rules must be clearly defined and followed. When the concerns are heard, the manager has to determine if any ethics and conduct code was broken. When that is done, the manager must take the appropriate corrective action.

Self-Accountability:

This is when a manager takes accountability for his or her actions. If the manager makes mistakes or breaks any rules or codes of conduct, he or she takes responsibility and owns the mistakes. This is an example of true leadership. This will ensure other team members follow suit. We are human, after all, and are bound to make mistakes but must learn from them. There should be a margin of error and a number of chances given before any exceptional action can take place.

Speaking up:

Influential leaders speak up for their teams and therefore command respect. Speaking up for your team means you stand by them, and they look up to you more for any concerns they have. They will stand by your side, and it allows you to nurture those ethical values that the business demands from them. You lead the way for these team members to grow and become ethical leaders. It fosters teamwork and mutual respect.

Practice the Preaching:

When you preach ethical values, you must stand by them and practice them. This is also part of leading by example, and every manager can set the standards. This is the way things will go because you set the rules, follow them, and ensure others do the same. You cannot just talk the talk and not walk the talk. You have to stand by your values and beliefs and adopt sound ethical values to earn and command respect.

There is a lot that goes into ethical leadership, and we covered the most essential aspects. Perhaps we may have just scratched the surface, but the point is to be a moral leader and ensure that others follow your example. You can go a long way as a leader and become highly effective at your skills as you grow in your career, make mistakes, and learn from them. You will eventually be a leader that is a guide, mentor, and innovator but also is accountable for your actions and willing to take responsibility for them and your own mistakes. There is no shortcut, but these several areas are ones you must focus on as a leader and manager. You will show excellent leadership and be an inspiration to everyone else around you.

Chapter 10:

Leading through Change and Uncertainty

As we wade through this chapter, you will understand the importance of leading through change and uncertainty in effective leadership and management. We have started the chapter by first examining the nature of change and uncertainty and their challenges. Secondly, the chapter discusses the essential qualities and skills a leader requires to lead effectively through change and uncertainty. This includes communicating clearly, providing direction and vision, and fostering a culture of resilience and adaptability.

Finally, you will understand practical strategies and approaches leaders can adopt to manage change and uncertainty effectively. Finally, the chapter explores the importance of leadership development and its role in equipping leaders with the skills and knowledge they need to lead effectively through change and uncertainty.

Undoubtedly, change is the only constant in life. We have to continuously change and evolve as per the circumstances. "Adapt and persevere" should always be the attitude. Leadership that is flexible can adapt and persevere regardless of the circumstances. Life is always so unpredictable. You can never expect anything. Therefore, leaders must have the foresight to see unexpected situations or curve balls. If you read previous chapters, you understood how leadership evolved during a pandemic crisis because that was an incredible and unexpected life curveball. One must always expect the unexpected. Uncertainty is challenging, but strong leaders can survive these situations because their experiences have taught them to be strong. As you will learn ahead, this is a trait that genuinely defines leadership because the true test of a leader is to lead in uncertain times.

Therefore, true leaders are those who possess the grit and resolve to handle any matter. As stated earlier, there are a few areas where they must excel, and they are as follows:

Clear Communication:

Communication is king, and leaders must be excellent communicators when it comes to leadership. They have to pull out all the stops and ensure that every instruction is crystal clear to their teams, whether it is through email, inter-office chat, or in person. You must lead by example and give feedback when needed. Everything should be clearly explained as you would want things presented to you. You have to show empathy in every process. In fact, this is something that applies to this and every area discussed from here on out. The communication should be set in such a manner that there is no room for rumors whatsoever. Since you are the boss and call the shots, lead the conversations clearly so there is no confusion, and request feedback if more clarity is required.

Providing Direction and Vision:

You must remember that your team looks up to you as a visionary, and they expect you to guide them in all situations, good and bad. Companies go through ups and downs, and sometimes tough decisions have to be made. In this situation, companies have to ensure the leadership goes the extra mile and in ensuring there is zero drama and chaos. They have to be effective communicators and guides and take their teams with them through crucial situations. It could be rightsizing or any other financial concern. Rightsizing is when companies reduce staff they feel is hurting their productivity and profitability or when they have over-hired and are unable to get the most out of the additional employees. Therefore, an evaluation of teams takes place, and companies offload those they feel are counterproductive. This is when those companies should make it clear to those left behind that their jobs are safe and secure. The one thing employees worry about is job security, and they stick to those companies and leaders who provide job security and value them.

Zoom, Google Meet, and Microsoft Teams were popular during the COVID-19 pandemic, and that was how leaders were able to communicate with teams effectively and remotely. The leader must set the way teams work remotely and monitor their progress. There should be checks and balances on every team member, including the leader too. Employees appreciate leaders owning their mistakes because this is what leading by example is all about. You inspire them to own their mistakes and learn from them.

Fostering a Culture of Resilience and Adaptability:

It is clear how each area is so very interconnected, and the same example would fit in all areas. This is where leadership counts. Leaders require foresight to ensure their teams can meet upcoming challenges. They have to prepare those teams to be resilient, flexible, and easily adaptable. Adapting and persevering, as stated earlier, should always be the mantra. There is no reason to be afraid because uncertainties and change are common and sometimes way too common. We cannot always guess what will happen, and those with the best foresight can make mistakes. The way it works is to learn from your mistakes, take notes, apply strategies that prevent those mistakes from reoccurring, and go for the win. Winning teams are those that are resilient. Business teams must work like team sports, where teams have to consistently face challenging circumstances and be prepared for anything. Those situations require teamwork and visionary leadership. The teams must have confidence in their leader that he or she will guide them through these uncertain times, and at the same time, they should know that they will deliver well on his expectations or exceed them.

As a leader, you must encourage groupthink and brainstorming between teams. Every team member should freely speak and come up with exciting ideas, and leaders should encourage more of the same. The best ideas can come from internal teams because there is a lot of talent and inspiration at hand, and capable team members must be given a chance to speak and suggest exciting and innovative ideas. Leaders must align their individual priorities with those of their companies, and those include company values, mission statements, goals, and objectives, and none of those should change whether there is a pandemic or business as usual.

Leaders must look at uncertainty and change as learning opportunities because they cannot possibly know everything. They are not blessed with crystal balls and can predict the future. They base their knowledge on experience and make judgment calls in those situations. There is never a right or wrong answer. You just take the situation as it comes and see the best strategy for that situation and add to your knowledge on how better you can tackle the same situation time and again as the need arises.

Teams appreciate leaders who show humility, transparency, and honesty. They also appreciate those who acknowledge their imperfections. One should not be too hell-bent on perfection; they lose sight of their core ideals and goals. No one is perfect, and that should be the rule of thumb in all business organizations. You have to keep reminding the team that we are all in this together and we can see the situation through no matter what. You should possess that iron will and resilience to deal with complicated situations. Get the team on board, have them chime in, and show that there is an "all for one and one for all attitude."

Unfortunately and fortunately, life is not mundane. Life keeps changing and evolving. Sometimes, we trigger changes, or sometimes, we have to face curveballs from anyone. There is never a right or wrong approach, but the right approach, according to the situation, is what is cost-effective and gets the job done with maximum damage control. Take the bulls by the horns, keep your team with you, brainstorm, and face all the challenges together. There should be immense team spirit and cooperation, and the true leader can ensure that happens all the time. Leaders must prepare their teams for uncertain times based on their experience, and that is where their leadership truly shines.

The best way to end this discussion and move to the next chapter is by the following:

"Expect the worst, and hope for the best. Lead like the man or woman of steel and take charge. Nothing is impossible, and learn from your mistakes. Wash, rinse, and repeat!"

Here is a fitting quote from Rocky Balboa (2006), where Rocky (Sylvester Stallone) explains to his son how to manage times of change and uncertainty. This is a rule that all leaders must follow, and that is where I end this chapter:

"Let me tell you something you already know. The world ain't all sunshine and rainbows. It's a very mean and nasty place, and I don't care how tough you are; it will beat you to your knees and keep you there permanently if you let it. You, me, or nobody is gonna hit as hard as life. But it ain't about how hard ya hit. It's about how hard you can get hit and keep moving forward. How much you can take and keep moving forward. That's how winning is done! Now if you know what you're worth, then go out and get what you're worth. But ya gotta be willing to take the hits and not point fingers saying you ain't where you wanna be because of him, or her, or anybody! Cowards do that, and that ain't you! You're better than that!"

Chapter 11:

Building Stronger Teams

This chapter discusses the importance of building strong teams for organizational success and the crucial role of leaders and managers in achieving this. Effective leadership and management practices are explored, including establishing clear goals and expectations, fostering collaboration and trust, providing opportunities for growth and development, addressing conflicts, and focusing on results. By investing in their teams, leaders and managers can create a culture of excellence that drives success and innovation. It starts from the leadership and spirals down to each team member.

The previous chapter depicted the way leaders should embrace change and tackle uncertain situations. This chapter builds on the same idea and speaks of building more substantial teams. A team is only as strong as its leader, but the leader needs his or her team to show strength too. While the leader could show resilience, the teams may not follow through. There should be a clear way that mental fortitude should rub off well on the teams. Here is a rule of thumb. Your team is your asset, so the more you invest in them positively, the better your return on investment will be. You do not have to think of this as a numbers game but as productivity, efficiency, and cost-effectiveness.

This idea of team investment leads me to the previous chapter's discussion on team sports mentality. There is no better way to build strong teams than by treating them as a sports team. It could be basketball, baseball, or soccer since teams work on a common goal to outplay and outsmart their competition and win. It also helps the team develop a winning mentality. That mentality plays a massive role in team development.

Establishing Clear Goals and Expectations:

That all being said, there are many ways to strengthen teams, and several of those are discussed in this chapter, but ensure that you understand that these are all based on the team sport mentality. That mentality is central to success. Those sports teams train together and discuss strategies. The head coach and team captain both outline the goals and objectives for each season and explain the strategy to accomplish them. Every team member's advice is taken and considered. When those goals are clear and adequately established, the team member understands his or her role and how that person would contribute to the overall team goals for that very season. There is no rocket science here because teams work like units. One can apply the strategies of a carefully coordinated battalion where the commander is very precise about the goals and the soldiers understand the orders pretty clearly. There is no ambiguity, and the message is clear in everyone's mind.

Very similarly, business teams also require clear instructions. The team leaders set the agenda for the fiscal year, and every member gets assigned a role to accomplish that based on their position in the company. Through well-coordinated efforts, those goals are achieved well before set deadlines.

Fostering Collaboration and Trust:

It is essential to know that the team in teamwork is the most crucial element. When it comes to sports teams, each player in the position that he or she is playing has to know their role and expect the same from others. The strategy has to be clearly explained and followed through. This brings in collaboration as the teammates depend on each other to score or defend a goal. The head coach and captain outline team formations, especially in soccer, and going off script will spell disaster. The formations are designed to suit the strengths of the team, and hence they should be followed, and one should take calculated risks. There should be strategies and counterstrategies, and those come with a sense of collaborative trust. Collaboration is everything because even in business, team members are assigned roles and have to work together to achieve goals. They trust in each other for doing their job right and are free to voice opinions, engage in active listening, and are open to receiving feedback. As long as these checkmarks are hit, the team works like a well-oiled unit, and the leadership has to nurture this level of teamwork.

Providing Opportunities for Growth and Development:

"Every champion was once a contender that refused to give up."

Rocky Balboa (Sylvester Stallone)

The above quote makes sense because all leaders were once entry-level team members who made it to the top by working hard and taking advantage of opportunities for growth and development. Leaders must provide all team members to learn and grow. These are the future leaders because they want incentives for professional growth. They want to grow with the team and the company. It could be through annual appraisals, workshops, or other training. Leaders should recognize those employees with solid potential and give them the opportunity to grow into higher positions. They need to have a strong eye for talent. Therefore, leaders give birth to future leaders, and that is the circle of life in business. Strong leaders avoid nepotism and favoritism and choose future leaders on merit, potential, experience, and performance. These are the proper criteria, and every leader should use these as a measuring stick no matter what kind of business they are part of.

Conflict Management and Resolution:

"Focus on the problems, not each other."

Every team has conflicts, and one has to rise above those to succeed. Leaders have to act as impartial and fair mediators. Every member needs to be treated as an individual, and both sides must be heard in a conflict. It is never about who is right or wrong but about the resolution. This is not about winning ego battles because there will never be a solution to conflicts. Crisis situations happen, and management under pressure is the true test of mettle. It gets worst when there are internal conflicts. Therefore, it is crucial to focus on the problems and not each other. Leaders must recognize that those individuals should be questioned on the issues at hand, and only then can both sides reach common ground. Both sides have to forgive, forget, move on, and work towards collaborative goals.

Result-oriented Approach:

A result-oriented approach is vital to team strength. While the journey is essential, it is a fruitless endeavor without the right results. Teams should focus on results and delivering their absolute best. There are no two ways about it because that is what management looks at. They look at results and numbers, and if they do not match, the teams will be put to task. This is where leaders should spearhead their teams into following a result-oriented approach and ensure that each team member is delivering as promised. The approach could be based on SMART goals which translate into specific, measurable, achievable, realistic, and time-bound. For example, one smart goal would be to achieve double sales and profits in the current quarter. Therefore, a SMART strategy should be outlined to achieve those specific results. This fits the criteria, and therefore, the results will come with the right approach.

The best teams are those that work together and rely on each other. Each member has strengths and weaknesses. Each member should work in a way where individual weaknesses are supplanted by individual strengths. They should think and work like champions and deliver their best. They should be strong, confident, and self-reliant, and the leaders have to instill that belief in them that their teams are winners. The recommendations outlined in this chapter are worth considering and practicing because they can turn contenders into winners. When they adopt that winning mentality, they become unstoppable!

Chapter 12:

Leading through Effective Communication

A s we move to this chapter on the importance of effective communication in management and leadership, we have initially discussed the role of communication in management and leadership respectively. Then, I shared the best practices for effective communication in management and leadership, including active listening, clear messaging, regular check-ins, and multiple communication channels. The final section covers strategies for overcoming common communication challenges such as difficult conversations, managing remote teams, and communication during crises. Overall, the chapter emphasizes the significance of effective communication for building strong relationships with teams, inspiring innovation, and achieving organizational goals. Let's get the ball rolling now.

Communication is undoubtedly key to effective leadership. A leader has to be an excellent communicator. Communication requires leaders to practice active listening effectively and clearly stating goals, objectives, and instructions on deliverables. If there is a fault in communication, then the burden of error falls on the communicator, which is the leader or manager and not the team member. We will cover many effective communication strategies for the modern leader and manager.

Active Listening:

Leading is not about delegating responsibilities and assigning tasks. It also involves listening and that too active listening. This means you must know when you should talk and also when you listen. It shows that you care about your team members' opinions, feedback, and ideas. Similarly, when they do respond with those, it is imperative to participate in that discussion actively. The way it works is to ask questions, request their collaboration and elaboration on their ideas, and then take notes on whatever feedback they provide. Team members appreciate active listening, and it goes both ways. They will actively listen to you when you speak and vice versa.

It is pretty essential to reside at the moment and refrain from interrupting your team members. Your focus should be straight ahead toward them and the conversation at that. This can be accomplished by removing distractions and perhaps putting your phone on silent or DND (do not disturb). These measures will allow you to actively listen to your team members' feedback, ideas, and opinions, and that is an example of impactful and excellent leadership.

Clear Messaging:

It would be best if you were very specific when giving instructions to employees. Those instructions should be clear and concise. For example, it is highly essential to describe the intended project result or any strategic endeavor with complete clarity on the deliverables by the time each milestone conclusion arrives. If those goals are not being delivered as planned, the communication could be further simplified. You could also request feedback from employees on how you can offer further clarity or assistance.

When you send clear messages to employees or team members, you reduce confusion centered on priorities. Each employee will adequately understand their progress toward the deliverables, and this will, in turn, increase their engagement in the process at hand.

Regular Check-ins:

Employee check-ins are pre-arranged meetings taking place between the manager and individual team members. It is an opportunity for both the manager and team members to have a one-on-one conversation on several areas regarding work and career progress. These should be ideally regularly held because it gives both parties an insight into how things are progressing, and the team member should be open to receiving guidance, support, and feedback from his or her manager.

These employee check-ins can serve as informal performance evaluations and a way for the manager to motivate the team member to give his best at everything and ensure that his or her job is safe. The team member can ask any questions or concerns openly and honestly without fear of being judged. This kind of communication can transform into performance discussions, keep motivation levels high, and reinforce work commitment.

Multiple Communication Channels:

Strong leaders must use a multi-tiered approach when it comes to communication. The different ways mentioned above act as channels. Active listening, regular feedback, and check-ins are all excellent ways to improve communication in the workplace. I would like to focus on team feedback here because that could help you become a better manager. You will build their trust by listening to their feedback because they will feel valued. It can help you grow as a leader, especially if you listen and act. It is more about walking the talk and just talking. Therefore, you should participate in active listening and hear their concerns and ensure you take action on it if you see fit. If you do not, you must have valid reasons why you are not implementing their feedback.

Feedback should be continuous and regular, and you must implement changes. Otherwise, you will lose credibility and trust as a leader. Your team will not look up to you because they also want to feel valued as much as you are a manager. At least, when you have credible reasons to back your actions, the times you do not implement their feedback, they will still feel respected because you gave them an ear and appreciated the feedback. You will still maintain your value, and they will also feel valued. The value and feedback system go both ways, so implement it well.

When it comes to multiple channels, assessing which works best for communication between your team and you is essential. Documenting deliverables, expectations, goals, and objectives is important because otherwise, there is no proof of what you want from them. Channels include emails, texts, and intracompany communications software like Microsoft Teams, Slack, Google Hangouts, and Discord. Remote communication can take place through any of these software or video conferencing programs like Google Meet and Zoom. It is always best to use official channels for team communication because unofficial channels cannot be considered at the time of disputes or conflict resolution.

In every corporate setup, managers have to make tough calls, including giving employees a whole lot of tough love. This also means they have to communicate difficult decisions when it comes to termination of employment contracts. Sometimes, working from home requires a different way to communicate because remote work does pose challenges. Some of those challenges have been discussed in previous chapters. This also requires effective and clear communication, and we will look at all the ways we will implement the tough calls.

Hangin' Tough:

Here is the thing. Tough calls are part and parcel of the workplace. Downsizing decisions, rightsizing initiatives, or employee terminations happen all the time. It is not easy to explain to any employee that their services are not required, but you can do it right and save face at the same time. Human resources/ HR policies should allow adequate severance pay of one to two months or more so that the laid-off employee has enough to survive until he or she finds the next gig. You have to respect the employee and thank him or her for services rendered during their tenure in the company. This is the best way for a send-off if the employee is leaving on good terms or is laid off due to rightsizing or downsizing or the politically correct term of company restructuring.

As a manager, you must explain the reasons carefully and let the employee know that he or she can count on you at all times for the need for a recommendation or any other documentation. You could even refer them to other places and get their foot in the door, and they will thank you later. This is the right way to do terminations or separations. In cases where the employee leaves on unfavorable terms or is dismissed for violating company rules and given enough chances, the manager should let HR handle the case. HR must request departing employees to give exit interviews if they are leaving on good terms. Exit interviews allow the HR team to explain better the reasons behind the departure and the employee's experience during his or her tenure.

When you want to hold on to employees, you must have a good heart-to-heart talk with them and explain that they are an asset to your firm and they should consider staying. If possible, you can have HR prepare a counteroffer to keep key employees at your firm. If the employee respects you and is loyal enough, he or she may stay provided they have not committed to the other company or accepted their offer of employment. It would be wise to keep your best human resources in your firm long term by providing regular professional growth and incentives. By constantly reminding them of their importance to the firm, they will continue to feel valued and want to stay with you long-term.

In the case an employee gets an excellent offer with professional growth and a salary you cannot match, you should not hold him back if the difference is too high. You should not stop employees' progress and let them leave on good terms. By forcing them to stay in these circumstances, they will lose morale and not perform for you the way they were doing previously. When favorable conditions exist at a later time, both parties could consider resuming their business relationship, and the chances of that increase tenfold if you do not stand in the way of their success.

In any crisis situation like close deadlines, and pandemic situations, team managers must hold their nerves and guide their teams in the best manner to achieve goals and targets. Even if the deadline is near, remote communication tools and constant updates within teams can help speed up deliverables. Everyone needs to put their heads together and get to it. The manager is as involved as the rest of the team and leads by example. There is a detailed discussion on pandemic leadership in previous chapters, so it is best to revisit those chapters to get a thorough understanding. As a recap, remote communication tools and regular team check-ins help a lot, no matter how spread out a team is. The communication has to be clear. Voice notes are helpful to clarify things and give a better context to situations.

The Curtain Call:

Communication is critical in business, and there can be chaos if there is zero clarity. Throughout this chapter, we understood the best ways to maintain effective communication with team members and how to keep them motivated throughout their career journey in your company. We also discussed making tough calls and how best to inform impacted team members. It would be wise to hold on to your best talent and the different ways to retain them. At the same time, it is imperative that we let them go if we cannot give them the professional growth another company has offered them because this will allow them to be thankful to us and even return to us later when conditions are favorable for both parties. Conflict management requires clear and concise communication through official channels, with everything adequately documented. Communication skills are a hallmark of any leader, may it be business or otherwise. If you keep in mind all the essentials discussed here, you can be a fantastic leader and communicator in no time at all.

Chapter 13:

Developing Effective Leaders and Managers

" **E** very champion was once a contender that refused to give up."
Rocky Balboa (Sylvester Stallone)

Leadership is a wonderful skill, and I have used this chapter to explore the importance of training and development in leadership and management. A well-designed training program can help individuals learn the skills and knowledge required to lead and manage effectively. Additionally, ongoing training and development can keep leaders and managers up-to-date with the latest trends and practices in their respective fields.

There are various methods of training and development that organizations can implement. These methods include on-the-job training, mentoring and coaching, classroom training, online learning, and leadership development programs. Organizations should start by identifying the skills and knowledge their leaders and managers need to acquire or improve. Providing ongoing support, feedback, and coaching is essential to ensure that individuals can apply what they have learned in their roles.

It is said that leaders are born and not made. This could be a misnomer because not all of us know about our innate leadership abilities until we discover them through experiences, whether those are educational or in the workplace. Sometimes, one can develop those skills through workshops, training programs, and on-the-job responsibilities. You can learn leadership by taking charge of clubs in school too. There are many ways one can lead, and there is no one-size-fits-all track to follow. How can one claim to be a leader or not without a self-evaluation? Sometimes, life puts you in certain situations where you have to take charge.

Organizations can identify and groom leaders in many ways, and we will go through those various ways so our business can figure out all the hidden talents among your employees who are just waiting to show what they can do. Some of them may be unaware of their capabilities and just need a push in the right direction.

Identifying Leaders:

A keen manager can identify leadership prospects through experience with different team members. All the manager needs to do is to see who takes the initiative on projects and shows a desire to lead. You can see solid people management skills in that individual, and you could choose that person for leadership training. You can give that talent a test run and see how well he does in a leadership role. If he meets or exceeds your expectations, you have got your man. Every individual has personalities that separate him from the rest. The idea is to be an excellent judge of character and talent. Identifying is the first step, but there is more to do when honing leadership skills in others.

Skill Development:

The managers in your business must be great at their job and lead teams successfully. However, that is only scratching the surface. You need to develop their skills further because they have to be prepared for any challenge and lead their teams in any crisis situation. Leadership in crisis is an actual test of mettle. You can be an excellent leader if you anticipate challenges and prepare for them in advance. You could be wrong, but at least you had the foresight to see that there is danger lurking around the corner. This is why skills development is essential. There are many ways to build skills in both new and experienced managers. One way is to invite professional coaches who have worked with organizations of various sizes and have them conduct workshops that cater strictly to your workplace environment. Those workshops, seminars, and training sessions must be made mandatory for every manager in the company and those you have identified as potential future managers.

Shadowing and Learning by Observation:

Another way to build skills in potential leaders is called shadowing. This means the manager plays a role of a mentor to the identified leadership talent and coaches him until he or she is prepared to take on that role. The training could be hands-on, where he or she is asked to take on projects, and you can observe how well they take on the challenges. Similarly, the talent can also observe you by spending time with you and see how you motivate team members and get them to deliver as and when needed. You can then quiz that talent on what he observed and how he or she would handle those same situations. These are the many ways shadowing can work because learning by observation is an excellent way to absorb leadership skills on the job.

Ongoing Support, Feedback, and Coaching:

You can never be perfect, but you can be a perfectionist. If it is your job to groom future leaders of a business, you take responsibility with pride and honor. There is no better feeling than mentoring talented team members and grooming them to take on successful manager roles. You feel validated as a leader because, after all, one facet of leadership is to offer guidance, coaching, and mentorship. These same mentees of yours will thank you because you guided them to success and, in many ways, passed the torch. They will learn from you and also become guides and coaches to other talented team members they lead.

As a leader, you have to constantly groom yourself because one day, you may own a business or be a CEO. The situations become more challenging, and you have to be prepared. This is why every business needs to support the grooming of every talented team member and manager to take on higher roles and climb up the proverbial corporate ladder. Feedback goes both ways. In the previous chapter, we discussed how feedback for the manager and team members are both equally helpful. You can always learn a great deal from your team members and vice versa.

The mentoring, guidance, and feedback should be pretty regular across all departments. Similarly, the training sessions and seminars should always continue. In fact, managers can also lead sessions instead of professional coaches on some occasions. You can also assign talented members tasks to lead some training sessions on areas they excel at. This will give them confidence and allow you to judge their leadership capabilities. It is an excellent idea to incentivize budding managers to push themselves because of the perks and benefits they may receive upon promotions. The obvious advantage is a better salary, but they earn a title in the company and are ready to climb up further in the company. Company vehicles, fuel allowance, and other perks are always expected, but the intellectual and emotional maturity they gain is priceless.

At times, it may also help to send some talented individuals on long-term training courses, certificate courses, and diploma programs. You can even encourage them to apply for and attend executive MBA programs by financing them. The skills and knowledge these individuals can gain can do wonders for your business if you allow them to apply them properly. They will be even more thankful that they earned an extra academic qualification due to your encouragement. There are many ways one can constantly groom future leaders.

The Leaders of Tomorrow:

Prospective managers are tomorrow's leaders, and they can take your company to greater heights because this helps with succession planning. When managers get to retirement age, they have the next generation ready to take over, follow in their footsteps, and perhaps bring something new to the table. As managers, we must prepare tomorrow's leaders because our business success depends on it. If you do not have any leaders groomed to take up higher management positions, you will have incompetent leaders take on those roles and drive your business into the ground.

Remember that you were also once a team member and groomed yourself to be a business owner, manager, or any leadership role. You had mentors and coaches, too, and now you have attained a position where you can do the same for your team members and pretty much pass the torch at the right time.

Chapter 14:

Women in Leadership

When it comes to women in leadership roles, a significant gap still needs to be addressed. This chapter will explore the challenges women face in leadership positions, the importance of diversity in leadership, and how women are breaking barriers and driving change.

Women face many challenges when trying to break into leadership positions. These challenges include gender stereotypes, unconscious bias, and a lack of support networks. Additionally, unconscious bias can lead to women being overlooked for promotions and other leadership opportunities.

While it may seem that women are progressing in the corporate world and taking up more executive positions, it is still pretty much a man's world. However, the accomplishments of women in the corporate world are a sign that there will be a fair balance in the near future if things go in the right direction. There have been plenty of excellent examples of women in leadership, whether it is business or politics. When you look at politics, no better example comes to mind than Hillary Clinton. She has been a mainstay in American politics for over two decades or more. She first started her political career as the First Lady of the United States as the better half of former two-time president Bill (William Jefferson) Clinton. In the last two decades or so, she has taken up roles of a New York senator and Secretary of State under the Obama Administration in his first term as president. She has therefore worn many hats. She also contested elections in 2016 against incumbent winner Donald J. Trump. It is not surprising that she had the highest popularity vote but lost the elections by Electoral College vote. She is a leading role model and example for budding women politicians all over the world.

Outside the United States, there are many examples of women leaders, including former Pakistani prime minister Benazir Bhutto, former Turkish prime minister Tansu Ciller, Bangladeshi prime ministers Sheikh Hasina Wazid and Begum Khaleda Zia, and former German Chancellor Angela Merkel. This is proof that women can play a massive role in politics, and more women should follow suit. I can say the same for businesses, and this is especially seen in global enterprises. PepsiCo hired Indian-born Indra Nooyi as CEO in 2006, and she stayed in that post until 2018.

Similarly, Hewlett Packard (HP) once had a female CEO known as Cara Carleton "Carly" Fiorina, who served in that role between 1999 and 2005. L'Oréal Paris (Pakistan) is well known for the inspirational female CEO Musharraf Hai. Stephanie McMahon has been one of the top executives in the WWE thanks to encouragement from her father and WWE founder and current executive chairman Vincent Kennedy McMahon. In fact, his wife Linda McMahon extensively supported him for many years in a senior management role since the earlier days of the former Titan Sports – home of the formerly known World Wrestling Federation and now WWE. Linda has taken up roles of president and CEO and served as the 25th Small Business Administration administrator under former president Donald J. Trump. These women have paved the way for future women business leaders worldwide. It is fantastic to see women step up and compete with men for leadership positions and break traditional gender roles.

That being said, there are several challenges women still face, and until they do not overcome these challenges, they will not be on equal footing as men in business leadership. Some of those are discussed as follows.

Gender Stereotypes:

Women have for a longer time seen as homemakers and full-time mothers, but thanks to 20th-century developments, they moved into professions like teaching and school administration. It was about time women entered the business world by earning business degrees and competing with men for top positions. Those gender stereotypes, however, remain in place in some parts of the world, especially in developing nations. However, if you see the examples of female prime ministers earlier, those were mostly from developing countries. In fact, Musharraf Hai was the CEO of the local wing of a global corporation in a developing nation, so there is hope for women, and many women have followed suit in that country. You would find them taking on several leadership roles. Almost all human resources professionals are women, so the business world is changing as we see it. Therefore, a grassroots change is taking place because the new millennium has brought greater awareness. Gender stereotypes must be thrown in the alleys of ancient history for women to progress globally in business.

Unconscious Bias:

There is an unconscious bias in the business world against women, where some women feel that they are paid less than men in similar positions or do not get as many growth opportunities. It is unfortunate because men still dominate business globally. It is possible that men feel threatened by women and fear that male domination in business will be reversed. That should not be the case because business positions and roles should be awarded on merit rather than gender.

This unconscious bias should end because the world has to progress, and this is a very ancient mentality of male superiority over women. There are excuses made by business owners that women get married and have children, and because of their dual roles as a mother and corporate employees, it becomes hard to manage both responsibilities. Women have successfully managed both roles, and they should be given their due appreciation. Apart from maternity leaves, women have demonstrated their presence and success in the business world.

The Lack of Support Networks:

Finally, women do not have the high support networks men afford. Most corporations are owned and run by men, and women find it hard to scale up. We should enable support networks for women because these incredible ladies are breaking barriers. They have shown that they can play the same field as men and sometimes way better than them. As said earlier, there has been progress, but there is still a very long way to go. Women require men's support to move up the corporate ladder, and all men should take up these initiatives very seriously. There could be some serious talent in women that could take corporations to much greater heights.

Today, if we ask anyone names of famous business leaders, we will come up with Bill Gates, Steve Jobs, Mark Zuckerburg, Jeff Eezos, Larry Ellison, Elon Musk, Jack Ma, and others. You do not see a woman's name here, and I hope that one day many women join this illustrious list of global business leaders. Women have to take the initiative to start international businesses, and the men they live and work with should encourage them to change the business world. If men can do it, then women can do the same. It is high time that women step up in the business world and stand on equal grounds as men.

For starters, we can overcome the three fundamental issues discussed in this chapter, and that can be a foundation where women can step up and finally mount their place in the business world. It is great to see examples of female CEOs, but we need more of such incredibly talented women. All men will truly appreciate their contributions to global business when that happens. Vince McMahon, for example, did it for his wife Linda and daughter Stephanie. Such initiatives can be taken up by other male CEOs and pave the way for women to succeed in the business world. I hope we see this paradigm shift go into full swing very soon, as it is already taking place. I believe it is pretty much only a matter of time before we see women on equal footing as men, but we all have to work together to make this happen.

More power to women as they prepare to be tomorrow's great business leaders!

Chapter 15:

Successful Case Studies

We are finally reaching the end of the book and have so far covered several critical areas pertaining to management and leadership. We will look back at previous chapter discussions in the final chapter, but this penultimate chapter offers something very exciting. This chapter delves into successful management and leadership in modern-day organizations. Through examining real-world examples from various industries, this chapter aims to give readers a deeper understanding of what it takes to lead a successful team.

As you read ahead, I have begun the chapter by exploring several case studies of effective management and leadership. By exploring these case studies, readers can gain insight into the specific strategies and techniques that successful leaders have employed in these industries.

After introducing these case studies, the chapter focuses on analyzing what makes these examples successful. This analysis explores successful leaders' key traits and characteristics, such as the ability to communicate effectively, the capacity for strategic thinking, and the willingness to take calculated risks. These are leaders we must follow and adapt their strategies in our daily lives, especially when it comes to making tough business decisions – a key element of business management.

Finally, the chapter concludes by highlighting several key lessons that can be learned from these case studies. These lessons touch on the importance of building solid relationships with team members, investing in employee development, and the need for leaders to be adaptable and open to change. Once all is said and done, we get to the very end, and that should wrap up the book pretty nicely.

A textbook and business book can only explain so much about theories and concepts, but nothing comes close to real-life applications than applying all the knowledge by yourself. We also can learn so much from real-life examples in the form of case studies. This is why you will see case studies in almost every textbook written for the past few decades. Thankfully, there are so many examples we can choose from when it comes to famous entrepreneurs. These entrepreneurs showed excellent leadership, management, and courage under fire. For these very reasons, I am truly honored to feature them in this chapter and book. Without further ado, let's get to it then!

Reed Hastings – Netflix:

Netflix is now a household name in video streaming and pretty much a common feature in all famous smartphones, smart television sets, laptop/ desktop personal computers, and more. Netflix did not start as a video streaming business but became a pioneer thanks to its roots in the home video business. Netflix was partially responsible for ending Blockbuster Video's reign as the top video rental enterprise in the United States and the world. Netflix started as a DVD rental by-mail company back in the late 1990s and became largely successful thanks to a very simple idea concocted by founder Reed Hastings.

In 1997, Reed Hastings co-founded Netflix with former Pure Software colleague Marc Randolph after trying his hand at computer software such as Pure Software. They caused a disruption in the video rental industry by introducing DVD rental by mail. DVDs were sent in small returnable envelopes, and for like $20 or so a month, you could rent two discs at a time and watch it for as long as you want without late fees that physical stores like Blockbuster

Video would charge. It became a massive success and gained a substantial amount of subscribers. The best part was you could build your queue on their website. As you returned one disc, the next one on your queue will be shipped out. This extended to Blu-ray discs eventually.

Blockbuster Video attempted this strategy by allowing discs and games to be returned to stores, but it did not become a success as it wanted. Blockbuster has folded today, and only one franchise store exists in Bend, Oregon. It is now ironic that Blockbuster Video once had the opportunity to buy out Netflix but did not consider them much of a player in the home video business. Blockbuster is no more, and Netflix is a major global player in streaming video. This was the perfect missed opportunity, and had Blockbuster capitalized on that opportunity, it may still have been in existence and transitioned into the streaming industry and perhaps even keeping most of its video rental stores alive and kicking. Alas, that was not to be!

Gamefly adopted the same model created by Netflix for renting out video game discs by mail and continues to do so today. In 2007, Netflix introduced Netflix Instant, which allowed streaming movies and series on a computer. That eventually grew into producing and distributing original shows and films post-2010s and into the 2020s. It has now become a video streaming giant and also bid farewell to the DVD rental side this year as DVD.com (owned by Netflix) was shut down. Reed, in fact, has been a former member of the board of directors of Microsoft and Facebook.

Reed Hasting designed an internal culture guide for Netflix employees so that everyone is aware of company culture. He has reportedly offered average-performing employees higher severance packages to ensure they keep working hard for the company. He has also eliminated sick leaves and vacation time, giving employees autonomy on when they want time off. These are pretty innovative management practices. The culture guide was available publicly online so that prospective employees know what they are getting into before applying for work at Netflix. One could say that these are some of the reasons why Netflix has thrived through different eras.

Reed was known to make calculated risks as it did with the original DVD by mail service and later venturing into streaming and launching original content. He recognized the potential that perhaps streaming is the future and is now facing competition from Amazon Prime, Apple TV+, and Peacock. Reed is a game changer, and it was his incredible leadership that guided Netflix to become one of the biggest streaming companies in the world, with a global membership amounting to billions. He is the CEO but reportedly owns just one percent of the company!

Jeff Bezos – Amazon:

Jeff Bezos founded Amazon in July 1994 and, in nearly 30 years, has turned it into an ecommerce and technology powerhouse. It had humble beginnings as one of the first online bookstores. As the years grew and the 90s became the 2000s, Amazon acquired CDNOW and added CDs to its growing catalog. It is still one of the biggest music CD sellers in the world. Amazon added everything to its ecommerce business, from clothing brands to electronics to even groceries. It became well known for its phenomenal customer service.

Amazon later ventured into internet services like website cloud hosting with AWS – Amazon Web Services. Amazon Prime Video became a significant competitor of Netflix's streaming services. Amazon seemed to have a philosophy of being a jack of all trades and successfully proved it to its competition. Amazon revolutionized Internet shopping and, in recent years, through Amazon Logistics, outsourced delivery to Uber-like drivers to ship items to customers. Amazon has expanded globally and can now be used in several companies around the world. Most of mainland Europe, the UK, and Canada have native

Amazon websites. Amazon has gained a tremendous foothold in India, going against local ecommerce giants like Flipkart.

Bezos wanted to conquer the internet and started with books, and Amazon today is thriving in multiple industries, and that too successfully. He caused a disruption in the book retail business, with Borders bookstores shutting down in September 2011, although the reason for Amazon causing it is reportedly disputed. The point is that Amazon conquered every industry it succeeded in and timed its entry superbly. Jeff Bezos is a visionary who has shown that you can achieve anything if you do it right and put your heart into it.

Mark Zuckerberg – Facebook/Meta:

What can one say about Facebook/Meta founder Mark Zuckerberg? Mark has revolutionized social media in ways no one has done before. Facebook in the early 2000s was just a small social network for Harvard students. Mark and a few friends founded it and, within a short span of time, expanded it to other colleges and universities in the United States, and it was not long before it became a widespread social network in the United States and the rest of the world. A college email address was initially required to register, and one could invite friends, but it eventually became open to everyone. Facebook has membership billions and constantly growing. The social network company would purchase photo and video sharing giant Instagram and instant messaging app WhatsApp.

Mark has turned Facebook into a popular mobile app and consistently released new features. Facebook recently rebranded its parent company into Meta, which was a way for Mark to tell the world they are entering the metaverse. It is an alternate reality powered by augmented reality hardware, and you can buy and sell property and run businesses. It was based on blockchain technology. It is a successor of sorts or a spiritual successor to Second Life, which was also an alternate reality where you would represent yourself with an avatar and interact with other avatars. Metaverse is still in its infancy, and Mark is dedicated to seeing what possibilities it can unfold. In one way, it can bridge communication gaps like never before. Mark Zuckerberg has encouraged an open office style of working, which is more commonplace these days and is often seen in the tech space in places like Google. It promotes a more relaxed environment and fewer barriers to communication between management and teams.

The metaverse potential remains to be seen, but there is surely no doubt that Mark Zuckerberg is an innovative entrepreneur who literally changed the face of social media as we see it today.

Steve Jobs – Apple:

Whether you love or hate Apple, the company is another Amazon and has attempted to conquer every space in technology. Steve Jobs and his friend Steve Wozniak founded Apple Computer in 1976 and have become a technology juggernaut for close to 50 years now. From the original Macintosh to the iMac, iPod, iPhone, iPad, Apple TV, iOS, Apple TV+, and iTunes. Steve Jobs did not have it easy when it came to running Apple. The Macintosh was the first PC to offer a graphical user interface (GUI). Steve reportedly got the idea from Xerox, and this was later adapted by Microsoft under Bill Gates when it developed Windows. Despite the Macintosh becoming a success in the 1980s PC boom, it could never dominate IBM and other PC manufacturers. Steve Jobs parted ways with Apple in 1987 and founded NeXTwhich was another technology company. He reportedly had issues with the way Apple was running things and decided it was time to go off on his own and see what he was capable of.

Steve Jobs would return to Apple in 1997 as interim CEO and later became the permanent CEO, and the rest is pretty much history. Apple would start its conquest of the PC market with the iMac desktops and Macbook laptop/ notebook personal computers. The predominant operating system was Mac OS which has seen several iterations since then. It is now known as the "mac OS."

During his time as Apple CEO, he oversaw the development of iTunes, iPod, iPod Touch, iPad, and iPhone. He passed away in 2011, but Apple continued its dominance in the tech and smartphone space into today. The iPhone was revolutionary and pioneered the smartphone industry. The iPhone is a lasting legacy of Steve Jobs, and it is one of the highest-selling smartphones today.

Steve Jobs showed how innovation at the right time can lead to success. Even though the iPhone has many competitors, it is still a very formidable phone and continues to sell like hotcakes.

Jurgen Klopp – Liverpool FC:

Jurgen Klopp's inclusion is an interesting one. If you recall from previous chapters how corporations and their teams should be led like sports teams, Jurgen hails from a team sport. He has been in soccer management for over two decades now after hanging up his boots as a player back in 2001. He has managed some of the world's biggest soccer clubs, including Germany's Borussia Dortmund and England's Liverpool FC, of which he is currently the head coach. The head coach is the American term for soccer/European football club manager. Under Klopp, Dortmund has won the German Bundesliga twice and the English Premier League and the UEFA Champions League with Liverpool on two separate occasions. They reached the final of the UEFA Champions League thrice and won once, and the two losses were against Real Madrid FC. In fact, the Premier League victory under Klopp came after 30 years which was a massive accomplishment. Not only that, Liverpool has come second multiple times during Klopp's tenure.

Each soccer club has a distinct philosophy, and Klopp wanted Liverpool to adopt a winning philosophy and mentality, implement the "gegenpressing" style, and improve the squad by bringing in players that suited that style. It was during this time that players like Sadio Mane, Mohammad Salah, Roberto Firmino, Thiago, and club captain Jordan Henderson thrived and became global stars. Jurgen Klopp maintained an excellent relationship with his squad and the media. Despite a somewhat disappointing season the previous year, the club feels optimistic under Klopp and remains determined to claw back its way to the top of the league table. Jurgen Klopp has always encouraged a "never give up" and "never say die" attitude among his squad. He is a true example of a leader and team player, and these skills can be applied in business or any other professional field. The only other soccer managers to perhaps best Klopp in recent times are Pep Guardiola (FC Barcelona, FC Bayern Munich, Manchester City), Jose Mourinho (Chelsea FC, Tottenham FC, Porto FC, Inter Milan), and the legendary Sir Alex Ferguson (Manchester United). The latter even wrote several books, including one on management called "Leading." One can learn a lot from these excellent head coaches.

Leading from the Front:

In this chapter, we have looked at some fantastic leaders who lead from the front and deliver. They led their companies to massive successes and showed how innovation, timing, and smart business can make you global power in business. We paid tribute to these incredible leaders and hopefully learned a thing or two from them.

We move to the final chapter on the next page, which will be a summary and recap of previous discussions and an excellent way to end the book. I hope you have learned a lot throughout this journey. It is not over yet, so get ready for one final lesson!

Chapter 16:

Future of Management and Leadership

Now that we have reached the end of the book, I have examined some of the predictions and trends experts believe will shape the landscape of leadership and management in the coming years.

One of the most significant changes we expect is a shift towards more collaborative and inclusive leadership styles. Another trend that is expected to gain momentum is the use of technology in leadership and management. Additionally, the changing nature of work will heavily influence the future of management and leadership.

Overall, the future of management and leadership will likely be characterized by collaboration, technology, flexibility, and a commitment to ethics and social responsibility. As the business world continues to evolve, it will be essential for leaders to stay ahead of these trends to remain competitive and successful.

Leadership has evolved throughout the years, and we have seen through the previous chapters how essential certain areas are. We looked back at different management and leadership styles, crisis management, managing under pressure, pandemic leadership, women in leadership, communication issues, and a whole lot more. Throughout these different areas, we learned how to be an effective leader and communicator and constantly expect the unexpected. It is essential to know all these skills and especially learn a lot from the case studies presented in the previous chapter to achieve success. All of these exceptional leaders are role models for the modern leader. They displayed all the skills that have been discussed in the previous chapters.

There are tons more that have not been mentioned, like Larry Ellison, Bill Gates, Elon Musk, and Jack Ma. Bill Gates and Mark Zuckerberg are notorious for being Harvard dropouts, but both became successful entrepreneurs. This by no means is an indication that one should not graduate from college because not all of us can be that lucky to have such a grand idea and capital to start a business. I would still suggest that one should at least graduate from college and consider an MBA program, too, if possible. That, combined with real-world experience, would be incredible because most colleges and universities globally have implemented real-world practical experience in their degree programs so that you can get a mix of theoretical and real-life expertise too.

It's a Small World, After All:

The world has gotten very small thanks to the internet and technology revolution. It is perhaps an indication that remote office environments will be the future because the COVID-19 pandemic proved it can work, and that too very successfully. Leadership and management styles will evolve to accommodate this change. It is very true that a paradigm shift is taking place, and remote workplace management is on the cards.

Leaders have to anticipate new trends and ways to optimize workplace environments and constantly innovate. There should be no stopping innovation because other rivals will catch up. The office environments must continue to stay open and hierarchical roles that are now considered very traditional and ancient should be dropped. Team members must be given full autonomy but must adhere to preset deadlines.

In fact, the agile business environment has shown to thrive in the technology space where meeting deadlines is absolutely crucial. Project management software like

Asana, Trello, and Jira has been very popular, and interoffice communication through Slack, Microsoft Teams, and Discord seems to be prevalent in the near and distant future. Video meetings and remote conferencing will continue to be held on Google Meet and Zoom.

Leadership styles will be more collaborative as managers will not be stuck behind separate rooms but instead will be sitting with their teams and working on projects together. They will lead by example because the more open an office environment becomes, the teams demand that their managers work with them so deadlines can be met on time and products can be launched as intended.

It is foreseeable to see a completely digital workplace, and that has been implemented in some places in the world. It may happen because it will reduce overheads and still allow a means of communicating with teams wherever they are. It will also cut down on commute times and gas spending. Team members will be involved in all management decisions, and they will be empowered to take projects head-on and learn how to manage them autonomously. They will receive guidance from managers, but their autonomy will teach them independence and responsibility, and can be groomed into future leaders.

Technology has already played a massive role in the modern workplace, and leadership styles have to be adapted to it. The modern manager must be well-versed with all the latest software, tools, and technologies and be aware of emerging technologies to optimize their workplaces better. It is an exciting future and high time when leaders and team members can sit at the same pace remotely or physically and collaborate on projects together.

The Last Word:

We have finally reached the end of the book! Thank you so much for being part of this incredible journey, and I hope you have learned some essential and exciting management skills. I hope you know now how the future is expected to shape up and how managers must adapt to the latest technologies and leadership styles.

I hope you enjoyed reading the book as much as I enjoyed writing it. I must urge you to read the book again and identify chapters that are important to you, and take notes. This book is a guide for anyone wanting to be a manager or current manager. This is for anyone wanting to start a business, and I hope it helps you on your entrepreneurial journey.

It is an honor, privilege, and pride for me to write this book, and a tremendous honor that you have read it because it makes me feel validated that all the concepts and ideas I have explained are reaching people globally and everyone is willing to learn. This is the best thanks I can get from readers as an author. I must say that while this is undoubtedly not goodbye, see you later.

I am encouraged to continue exploring more ways to teach exciting leadership ideas, and perhaps the next one will be a continuation of this chapter. We can all learn how to prepare for the future and best use technology to our advantage and improve our leadership styles. The future is exciting, and by predicting and being prepared, we can face the future head-on and be fully ready for the challenges that lie ahead.

Thank you all once again, and I hope to see you on the next journey!

www.ingramcontent.com/pod-product-compliance
Lightning Source LLC
Chambersburg PA
CBHW040854210326
41597CB00029B/4846